LORDSHIP GENEROSITY

GIVING ALL TO THE ONE WHO GAVE ALL

Matt Tullos & G.B. Howell, Jr.
with Tod Tanner

LORDSHIP GENEROSITY

ACKNOWLEDGMENTS

Cover & interior graphic design: James Wilson
Editor: Tammy Harris

LordshipGenerosity.com

Copyright © 2024

All rights reserved.

ISBN: 9798990266506

Unless otherwise stated all Scripture verses quoted are from the Christian Standard Bible ®, Copyright © 2020 by Holman Bible Publishers, used by permission.

To our friend & mentor, Henry Webb.

CONTENTS

THE BIG QUESTION	11
1 **THE BALANCE OF YOUR TIME**	19
2 **THE EXPRESSION OF YOUR GIFTS**	41
3 **THE STEWARDSHIP OF YOUR FINANCES**	69
4 **THE CLEANING OF THE SLATE**	91
5 **THE STORY OF YOUR LIFE**	115
6 **THE IMPACT OF YOUR LEGACY**	127
EPILOGUE	142
SPIRITUAL GIFTS INVENTORY	147
GROUP DISCUSSION GUIDE	152

FOREWORD

As a top student at Cambridge, Charles personified success, talent, intellect, and strength. He grew up in a family of wealth and privilege. Many fans considered him one of the greatest cricket players of his generation, a sport that was at the height of its popularity. Despite all these incredible circumstances, he made a courageous choice. In his early twenties, he surrendered everything to the Lordship of Christ- his life, his destiny, his story, his heart, and his fortunes. Imagine if he had just decided to play cricket and enjoy life here on Earth. Few would have remembered him. Besides, who can name one cricket legend? Yet historians for years will look back on the life of Charles (C.T.) Studd and his remarkable journey of daring faith and obedience. C.T. Studd dared greatly. He was a part of "The Cambridge Seven," young men who were some of the first Christians to reach into the heart of China with the gospel. Perhaps you've heard these words: "Only one life, 'twill soon be past, Only what's done for Christ will last." They were written by C.T. Studd.

Certainly, we aren't all called to the mission field, but we are all called to surrender to the Lordship of Jesus. This is the heart of *Lordship Generosity*. It is an openhanded call for us to surrender our riches, our time, our spiritual gifts, our story, our relationships, and of course our lives to Jesus.

It's our hope that as you read this book and consider the trajectory of your life, that God will bring you into a crystal-clear understanding of life lived to the fullest, once you surrender everything to the Lordship of Christ.

The concept of *Lordship Generosity* has impacted my life in more ways than I could have ever imagined. As an 18-year-old freshman college student at William Carey College in Hattiesburg, Mississippi with no family resources to fund for my education, I remember receiving an unexpected scholarship from First Baptist Church, Laurel, Mississippi for ministerial students. I didn't know those people, nor was I affiliated with anyone from that church. I wasn't even a student from Mississippi, but those generous people that I didn't even know, invested in me.

I've pastored some of the most generous people on this planet. Then, God called me to be a steward over the missional generosity of Tennessee Baptists. I've met so many believers who loved relentlessly, served tirelessly and gave sacrificially. In every chapter of my life, I've seen the generosity of God's people do the impossible, simply because they surrendered every part of their lives to the Lord.

More than a book,

- *Lordship Generosity* is a process. We dare you to search the Scripture and seek the Lord as you consider the content.
- *Lordship Generosity* is a mirror. We invite you to reflect on your life and ask God to give you a clear understanding of your place in His story.
- *Lordship Generosity* is an encounter. We invite you to bathe the process in prayer. Ask God to allow you to experience Him in every aspect of your life.
- And finally, it is a joy! *Lordship Generosity* has the potential to fill you with infinite joy as you release your life into God's hands and experience freedom from obsessive thoughts, worries, habits, and unrealistic perceptions.

In July of 1931, there was a celebration in Heaven as C.T. Studd finished his journey on Earth. The last word he spoke was a simple "Hallelujah." Wouldn't it be great if you made it to the end of your life, knowing that you surrendered everything to Jesus. No regrets. Nothing held back. I believe we'd all say, "Hallelujah!"

Dr. Randy C. Davis
President & Executive Director
Tennessee Baptist Mission Board

THE ONE BIG QUESTION
IS JESUS LORD?

LORDSHIP GENEROSITY

THE ONE BIG QUESTION

Is Jesus Lord over everything in your life?

Therein lies the key that opens all doors.

If you confess with your mouth, "Jesus is Lord," and believe in your heart that God raised him from the dead, you will be saved (Rom. 10:9).

This is the foundation of our faith. If Jesus isn't Lord of your life, you are just playing religion. If He is the Lord of your life, you have the opportunity to experience life in abundance. You'll experience abundance in peace, fulfillment, spiritual growth, wisdom, and love. In other words, the good stuff. The stuff that can't be taken away. The stuff the lasts long after we "shuffle off this mortal coil," as Shakespeare said. These are the things we all should be collecting.

We hope you think of *Lordship Generosity* as a process to help you take an inventory of how you are responding to the lordship of Jesus. It's not just about your money. Through this study you'll be challenged to look at your entire life. Just to stop for a season and look at where you've been, where you are, and where you were going as a believer.

NOTE: THIS IS DIFFICULT.

We have many distractions and responsibilities in our hurried lives. Just stopping sometimes doesn't make any sense. We have been programmed to keep going, keep plowing, keep pressing on, keep hustling. Make no mistake, hard work is important; but misappropriated hard work and management ultimately will lead to a life of regret. This is so important! Your decision regarding Lordship will ultimately impact so many lives.

God has called us to live mindfully.

LORDSHIP GENEROSITY

"For which of you, wanting to build a tower, doesn't first sit down and calculate the cost to see if he has enough to complete it?" (Luke 14:28). This is the primary message of this little book. You and only you can judge the peace that you have in your life. As the Holy Spirit guides you on this journey, we believe that in time, you'll discover and celebrate a new change that comes from self-reflection. But ultimately, you'll be changed by the Holy Spirit and His power in your life. He is the change agent. This is not a program of self-improvement or motivational stories. It's a clarion call to allow the Holy Spirit to do His work so you can achieve and celebrate His work in your life. This type of celebration flows out of gratitude and generosity as a response to what God has done in you.

If you aren't mindful of your life, you'll be amazed at how swiftly it can pass through your fingers. Perhaps you've had the experience before. You go to the grocery store to get the gallon of milk, but once you walk in you are bombarded by a million other items: dog food, apples, bread, cinnamon, chicken, pudding cups, juice boxes, crackers, and, and, and. After 15 minutes, you have a full cart and step up to the register. Only then do you realize you forgot what you came in for — the milk! We can be so transfixed by all the shiny objects we encounter that we forget the most important thing. So, what is that one thing? It's to live a life of total surrender under the Lordship of Christ. Everything else is second best.

To live generously under the Lordship of Jesus Christ allows us to experience a volitional surrender to His grace and purpose. It's a relief when we consider the awesome wisdom and power that God displays when a believer totally surrenders and gleefully hands over the reins of his or her life to the infinite — to the powerful and sovereign Savior.

We believe that Jesus Christ is the Lord of all creation and we're called to submit to His authority and rule in our lives. Jesus is not only the Savior of the world, but also the ruler and master of all those who follow Him. The idea of Lordship is rooted in the biblical teachings that Jesus is the Son of God and that He has been given all authority in heaven and on earth. In the New Testament, the apostle Paul wrote that *"if you confess with your mouth, 'Jesus is Lord,' and believe in your heart that God raised him from the dead, you will be saved"* (Rom. 10:9).

This confession of faith in Jesus as Lord is considered a fundamental aspect of Christian belief. Living under the Lordship of Christ involves acknowledging Him as the ultimate authority in one's life and seeking to follow His teachings and example. This includes radical obedience, revolutionary love, and relentless service to others as He did. That is our generous response to His lordship. Our sole purpose is to please Him.

DON'T BE A WIND CHASER

Throughout the course of his life, Malcolm worked diligently. He religiously obeyed all the wisdom of his financial advisors. He saved 20% of everything he made. He often lived below his means. He prudently studied every financial investment. He worked his way up the organizational chart, and after 40 years working for the same start up, he finally found himself seated at the desk as CEO. But being a CEO of an exciting company was not the end all for Malcolm. Everything he did was to get him to the day when he could pack it in and live his dream on a tropical island with great sunsets and frozen margaritas in the evening.

When the day finally came, Malcolm consolidated all of his assets into a low-risk fund, boxed up his personal items, and left for his great retirement adventure. It's the American dream, isn't it? Many considered Malcolm a wise and scrupulous manager of wealth. Honestly, who wouldn't want to have enough in their portfolio to live off the interest?

As he wheeled out of the parking garage for the last time, a drunk driver ran through a red light, careening into his Mercedes.

By the time the ambulance arrived, his life was over. What seemed to be a genius plan actually turned out to be empty and meaningless. Malcolm really hadn't thought about eternity, and now he was faced with a solemn understanding that he had missed the whole point. Now all that was left on this Earth, which he loved dearly, was the contentious division of his wealth among his miserable, long-since neglected children. As a billionaire king famously wrote, *"Absolute futility. Everything is futile. — a pursuit of the wind" (Eccl. 1:2,14).*

> **"If we live an intentional life, day by day, trusting in God's providence, and in His resources, ultimately the compounded interest of joy is infinite."**

Whenever we chase after security, we fail to live a life of adventure and purpose. In the end, none of us want to be wind chasers. Malcolm missed the whole point!

As believers, we know there is another way. It's an opportunity to live every day for The Day — to invest our lives in things that will never fade. As we walk through this study, we hope that you will choose to live, celebrate, and invest for your 10,000th birthday rather than your 65th. Most people find it hard to wrap their brains around that kind of living. We have a hard enough time getting through the week, and yet there is a dichotomy in the formula. If we live an intentional life, day by day, trusting in God's providence, and in His resources, ultimately the compounded interest of joy is infinite.

All change begins with self-evaluation. The first statement Isaiah made when he encountered the glory of God was: *"Woe is me for I am ruined because I am a man of unclean lips" (Isa. 6:5).*

Look at your life, your motives, and your activities. This is practical wisdom. *"The sensible person's wisdom is to consider his way" (Prov. 14:8a).*

Still, a self-examination must be done through the lens of grace. Jerry Bridges in his book, *The Gospel for Real Life* put it this way:

"We should never be afraid to examine ourselves. But when doubts do arise, the solution is not to try harder to prove to ourselves that we are believers. The solution is to flee to the cross and to the righteousness of Christ, which is our only hope. And then, having looked to Christ alone for our justification, we can look to His Spirit to enable us to deal with those areas of our lives that cause doubt."[1]

Our hope is that *Lordship Generosity* will help you appraise and navigate through the four biblical concepts of Lordship in your own life:

- Your Time
- Your Spiritual Gifts
- Your Financial Wisdom
- Your Emotional Health
- Your Personal Story
- Your Legacy

When Jesus is Lord in these six areas, your life transcends. It will make your life infinitely more meaningful and eternal. Your response to His lordship is generosity in every area of life.

CHECK OUT THIS
OVERVIEW VIDEO BASED
ON THIS CHAPTER!

LORDSHIP GENEROSITY

Note: At the end of each movement there are personal questions to consider. These questions are for you and you alone. In other words, they shouldn't be considered discussion questions. They're personal promptings for you and perhaps for your accountability partner. You might not be able to consider all these questions in the same week. That would be a lot! You might want to spread this activity out over a few weeks. They will help you make an inventory of your progress toward Lordship Generosity. Feel free to photocopy these pages so that you can review them frequently in the future. The PDFs of these pages are provided on the website.

CAPTURE THIS QR CODE TO GO TO THEM NOW OR VISIT

LORDSHIPGENEROSITY.COM.

MOVEMENT 1
THE BALANCE OF YOUR TIME

What could you do with 1,692 hours every year? It sounds like a dream, doesn't it? Our lives are so high capacity, it seems. It's hard to squeeze in all that we need to do within a day. The expectations are so high. Our family needs are pressing, and yet 1,692 hours represents the amount of time most Americans spend watching television. You have to wonder sometimes what our pets think as they see us staring into a noisy box for a vast majority of our time in the evenings. Keep in mind, this is not a call for all of us to start a big bonfire with our flat screens and projectors and computers and iPads. However, it's important to realize the priorities that we have embedded in our lives. A study in March 2023 reported the average American spent seven hours and four minutes staring at a screen each day. Americans spent three hours of that on their smartphones.

So how do we spend our time? As believers, does our time management look any different than those who have no faith in Christ? Why are we, as a society, so afraid of silence? Why is it that we can't turn off the noise makers in our lives? You might say, "OK, but we're multitaskers!" But in truth, are we really multitaskers or are we just a crowd of content consumers?

Time is as precious as money. As has been said: *Time is God's gift to you, and what you do with the time you have is your gift to God.* Time is a limited resource, isn't it? Being a good manager of time reflects a devotion to God and an understanding of the purpose of your life. Jesus told His followers, *"We must do the works of him who sent me while it is day. Night is coming when no one can work"* (John 9:4). He was reminding them of the nature of time. It's in limited supply, thus seizing every day's potential is important. Perhaps the thought of that stresses you out, but keep in mind that Jesus valued all aspects of time including rest. It's interesting to note that Jesus' ministry lasted a mere three years, and yet He accomplished so many things! Never once do we sense a frenetic pace. Jesus knew how to make the most of His time while He also embodied a deep sense of purpose and serenity in the angriest of storms. You'll never read this in Scripture:

Thus, Jesus hurriedly got up, realizing what an important day this was going to be. He ran to Galilee, and there He created 13 lesson parchments, visited 15 lepers, and had a confrontation with Judas who wasn't behaving and in whom He feared greatly. Hitherto, Jesus went in haste to the zealots committee where He talked for three hours. He encountered many voice messages from the throngs of Judeans and tried to return all of them with at least a beatitude or a warning. Exhausted, the disciples verily tried to keep up with the Son of God, but nay, they could not.

THE 4 W'S

So how will we think of time as we plan our day? Maybe it would be helpful to look at time the same way reporters journal the news. You've probably heard of the 4W questions; these work well as a lens to look at our time and to make decisions that will ultimately lead us to a more fulfilling and purposeful life. The 4W questions are: What, Where, Why, and Who.

The following exercise only takes a moment, but it could prove very valuable to those who want to make the most of their days.

WHAT?

What are the big items on your radar today? If you haven't done so already, make a list of the things you want to accomplish. Pray over the list and ask God to give you success as you make room for important things. Every day has certain surprises; we can't get around them. But if you're scrupulous with your time, the less chance you will have to be distracted or deterred from the things you wish to accomplish. At the end of the day, celebrate and journal the things you accomplished and prepare for tomorrow. Maintaining margins in your life allows you more opportunities to be generous with your time.

WHERE?

Where are the locations for the day? Begin your day asking God to give you safe travel and effective opportunities of influence in your path. To step into the providence of God means being at the right place at the right time. To live without a mindfulness of "where" does exactly the opposite. Without the Holy Spirit, we could find ourselves in the wrong place at the wrong time. Appealing to God for direction ultimately allows us to enter into His rhythm along the way. The book of Proverbs teaches that a person's heart plans his way, but the Lord determines his steps (Prov.16:9). Our simple daily prayer should be, "Lord, determine my steps." The Father is deeply interested in the places we go throughout the day. And He gives us this promise:

I will go before you
  and will level the uneven places;
I will shatter the bronze doors
  and cut the iron bars in two.
I will give you the treasures of darkness

and riches from secret places,
so that you may know that I am the LORD.
I am the God of Israel, who calls you by your name.
— Isaiah 45:2-3

WHY?

Why is probably the most important question of all because we often get tangled in activities and commitments before we ever prioritize. Having a clear understanding of your personal mission will help you as you deal with the details and activities of your life. Knowing our "why" helps us look forward to the opportunities of today. When we ask why, concerning our activities, we have the ability to be driven by purpose rather than the loudest voices we encounter. Ultimately, your purpose is a response to His lordship and our generosity of time. We see this focus in Paul's letter to the Philippians when he wrote: *"Brothers and Sisters, I do not consider myself to have taken hold of it. But one thing I do: Forgetting what is behind and reaching forward to what is ahead"* (Phil. 3:13).

"When we ask why, concerning our activities, we have the ability to be driven by purpose rather than the loudest voices we encounter."

"You're not Superman, you know."

As you budget your time, keep in mind that you aren't superhuman! We all are just ordinary people empowered by an extraordinary Savior. Here's a simple acrostic to help us balance our time well. We call this the P.E.O.P.L.E. Plan:

Plan Ahead

Planning your day can help you be more productive and efficient. Here are some steps you can take to plan your day effectively:

Planning ahead is as simple as starting a list. Make a to-do list of everything you need to accomplish during the day. Make sure your goals are achievable within the timeframe you have set for yourself. Assign specific times for each task on your list. Be sure to allocate enough time for each task based on its importance and complexity. Focus on one task at a time and complete it before moving on to the next one. If you know you are more productive at a particular part of the day, plan on putting your most challenging item during that time. This will help you accomplish what is your highest priority for the day. Contrary to what many people think, recent studies have shown that trying to multitask can be counterproductive and lead to a decrease in overall productivity. At the end of the day, review your plan and see if you accomplished everything you set out to do. If not, identify the reasons why and adjust your plan accordingly. Lordship *always* sets the plan!

> **"Multitasking is a major misunderstanding in productivity."**

Evaluate your Time

Take a close look at how you are spending your time on a daily and weekly basis. What has taken the most of your time at the end of that day or week? How does this activity line up with your priorities? These are the types of questions you'll want to answer when evaluating your time. You may come up with some questions that are your own that apply to your particular or unique life situation. It won't take you long to begin to see the benefit of evaluating how you spend your time. You'll soon find that taking a quick moment of introspective thought every night will help you prepare for the next day and the challenges you know you'll face.

One Thing at a Time

Multitasking is a major misunderstanding in productivity. So many times, we fall for the illusion that we could do more if we do multiple things at the same time. For the vast majority of people, especially guys, that just doesn't work. It's best to focus on one thing before moving on to the next. Otherwise, we become frantic plate spinners, constantly dashing from one wobbly plate to the next.

Prioritize Tasks

To make the most of your time, always prioritize the big rocks over the minutia of details. Ask yourself what the non-negotiables are and focus on them first. The more you prioritize your tasks, you become more productive and a better steward with your time.

Leave Margin

Margins are the guardrails of our day. If we fail to leave space for rest and recreation, we will live a life of self-defeating activity. Leave time to take a break. Many times, what you will find out is that during these times of Sabbath—even if it only means 15 minutes away from the task—you'll often find new inspiration and ideas. God created the brain with an amazing subconscious potential to work through issues, ideas, and problems, even while we are not consciously on the task.

Margins need to be practiced and protected. For some, this

seems counterintuitive. To step away feels like we are out of the game. It makes us feel selfish. Jesus frequently stepped away. *"Very early in the morning, while it was still dark, he got up, went out, and made his way to a deserted place; and there He was praying. Simon and his companions searched for Him, and when they found Him they said, 'Everyone is looking for you'"* (Mark 1:35-37).

This verse sounds familiar to most leaders. Our trip to deserted places away from everything, can cause stress for others, but ultimately you will bless them when you take a step back. We may initially wonder how people will get by without us, but surprisingly they do just fine! As Larry Eisenburg famously said, "For peace of mind, resign as general manager of the universe." When we have margin, we leave room for the Lord's interruptions.

 Eliminate Distractions

Often our greatest tools are the off buttons and the mute switches! Eliminating distractions will help us focus on being present. We all have a tendency to cry "squirrel" when there are noises and images that interrupt our work. If you fail to eliminate distractions, you'll become stuck in the morass of details we experience on a daily basis.

These P.E.O.P.L.E. questions will help you evaluate "why" you do what you do in fulfilling your personal mission—and why you should be doing certain things and not others.

WHO?

- Who are the people that you will encounter today?
- What kind of influence could you have in their lives?
- How could you bless the people you meet today?

As you begin your day, consider the number of people you will encounter. Perhaps you will meet people that challenge or even irritate you. Don't you think it would be good to be prepared before you meet them? As you begin the day in prayer, ask God for opportunities to bless and influence those you will encounter.

We see this in the journey of Samuel as he sought God's man to anoint as king over Israel. Samuel asked this "Who?" question as he surveyed Jesse's sons and sought for the one God had chosen. We look at Samuel and see that he had the same kinds of questions we encounter on a daily basis and that he totally relied on God for wisdom. Samuel's default choice would have been incorrect: *But the Lord said to Samuel, "Do not look at his appearance or his stature because I have rejected him. Humans do not see what the LORD sees, for humans see what is visible, but the LORD sees the heart"* (1 Sam. 16:7).

> **"If we invest in stocks, they will ultimately be liquidated. But when we invest in people, we are making a life-long AND an eternal impact."**

Questions to ask each day:
- Who needs my attention today?
- What are the needs of the people I encounter?
- How can I make the best use of my time with my family and friends?

The Bible continually reminds us that investing in people is an eternal undertaking. If we invest in a car, it will break down. If we invest in stocks, they will ultimately be liquidated. But when we invest in people, we are making a life-long AND an eternal impact.

Matt's Story of Mentoring

I don't think he'd ever remember this, but a man changed my life in a very intentional way. His name was Phillip Willis. Every Tuesday, Brother Phil (as we called him) would pick me up after school to take me to visit and evangelize other students. To this day, I still remember those visits. I remember watching Bro. Phil sharing his faith and challenging me to do the same. He was a busy man, but he decided to make an investment in me, and he changed the arc and direction of my life that year. He's my favorite example of a disciple who made disciples because I was the recipient of a man who took time to pour his life into an awkward ninth-grade boy. Discipleship requires investment—but the returns are eternal.

Here are six dynamics of a disciple-making disciple. They form an acrostic for the word INVEST. These dynamics help us turbo-charge our generosity of time and so that we can make an eternal impact on others.

I | Imitate Jesus.

Before the Sermon on the Mount, before water became wine, and long before the Great Commission was spoken, Jesus made disciples. He didn't begin by starting a class, giving a reading assignment, or testing the depths of men's spiritual potential. He began by simply saying, "Follow me." In other words, come see how I live, what I value, and where I go. This was the beginning of the process. Just come along and let's see what happens. Indeed, there are lessons to be learned and words to be said, but the beginning of discipleship begins with an invitation to follow. There are no badges, certificates, or hierarchy because we are all in process when it comes to discipleship.

N Name your person.

Discipleship isn't a large-group process. It's an intentional relationship. The exceptional disciple-maker is one who finds someone to invest time with. It's a running theme throughout the Bible.

Moses named Joshua and Aaron.
Paul named Timothy.
Elijah named Elisha.
And of course, Bro. Phil named Matt.

Who's the one you're going to pour your life, experience, skill, and prayers into? Hopefully, at least one name comes to mind as you're reading this. Name your person and make a commitment to make an investment.

V Value the relationship.

We sacrifice for the ones we value. The discipleship process implies sacrifice and sharing. It's got to be a priority. I have to confess, as an introvert, it's much easier for me to go it alone in ministry. I have to work hard at this. But we're much more effective when working alongside someone else. It sharpens our focus and makes us more intentional. As Solomon reminds us, *"Two are better than one because they have a good reward for their efforts"* (Eccl. 4:9). He also said, *"The one who has knowledge restrains his words, and the one who keeps a cool head is a person of understanding"* (Prov. 17:27). Jesus challenged us to be disciples who make disciples, who make disciples. Sounds repetitive, but this is the plan for discipleship. It is all about relationships and the lessons learned and then shared with others along the way.

E | **Encourage vulnerability.**

One of my favorite scenes in the Spielberg classic, "Jaws" is when the sheriff, the marine biologist, and the boat captain hunker over a table and begin to reveal their scars and their stories. There's something going on in that scene (besides the foreboding battle with a gigantic Great White looming in the next scene). It's these guys sharing their failures, setbacks, and adversities of the past. As disciples, we don't hide our battle scars. We learn from them and pass on the lessons. Many believe scars are to be hidden, not revealed—mainly due to what we call "shame." Jesus always uses our scars for His glory if we are courageous enough to be vulnerable.

S | **Set aside time.**

If we are serious about discipling others, we have to be willing to sacrifice time. If you're like most, time is like money. There never seems to be enough of it to invest. But we must set aside some time if we are going to be making disciples.

Reading the Gospels, it's amazing to see the number of miracles and holy, life-changing interactions Jesus had while He was on the way from one place to another. We never see Jesus checking the time and saying, "Sorry friend, I just don't have time. It's not on my agenda for today." He never scrolls through his calendar parchment and concludes, "I just don't have the time for this." He made time. We have to make time to disciple.

T | **Trust the process.**

The Philadelphia 76ers adopted this as their theme a couple of years ago. The owners of the team told their legions of beleaguered fans, who had suffered through season after season of losing campaigns, to trust the process. It even went so far that fans started chanting during the games, "TRUST THE PROCESS!" They nicknamed their all-star center, "The Process." Some thought it was hokey, but this is something disciple-makers must do. Trust the discipleship process. It's not an overnight thing and it's hard to measure results, but a continual investment of our lives into new believers, struggling friends, and the next generation will ultimately win out. It's gradual, but it's eternal. And if we intentionally invest in people, the process works if we work the process.

And one other "Who" question that takes courage and commitment: Who do I need to resist? That's a difficult one. Nehemiah provides an excellent example of a man who wouldn't be distracted by the nagging voices of inaction, diversion, and even criticism. God had called Nehemiah to rebuild the walls of Jerusalem; but, as in any great work, opposition raised its head. These time drainers wanted nothing more than to cause Nehemiah to delay and waste his time by demanding that he explain his actions and calling.

> *When Sanballat, Tobiah, Geshem the Arab, and the rest of our enemies heard that I had rebuilt the wall and that no gap was left in it — though at that time I had not installed the doors in the city gates — Sanballat and Geshem sent me a message: Come, let's meet together in the villages of the Ono Valley." They were planning to harm me. So, I sent messengers to them, saying, "I am doing important work and cannot come down. Why should the work cease while I leave it and go down to you?"*
> *– Nehemiah 6:1-3*

All of us have Sanballats and Geshams in our lives. They are the wrong who! They are not the ones who deserve our attention. You'll need to ignore the voices that intentionally or unintentionally seek to knock you off your call. It's imperative for us to discern who our Sanballats and Geshams are. Having a hard time identifying yours? James reminds us that whoever lacks wisdom should ask God for it. Ask Him for His help; He will reveal who your distractors are. Why does this matter? Because when we are involved in what God wants us to do, it's important for us to identify our potential distractors, especially when we are involved with discernment decisions. Remember, God has called us to love everyone, but not appease everyone.

> "Remember, God has called us to love everyone, but not appease everyone."

As you ask yourself these important questions: What, Why, Where, and Who, you'll want to consider the "absolute eternals." What am I doing with my time that will have eternal impact? This question isn't just about the monumental, super-duty, earth-shattering achievements. It may be a phone call to a discouraged friend, the extra 30 minutes when you get up to pray, or the Gospel conversation you have with the next-door neighbor as you're helping him debug his wi-fi garage door. Absolutely, these acts can have eternal impact!

We should never overfill our lives at the expense of missing the Aha! moments that are waiting in the wings. When we fail to plan our work, when we fail to budget our time. When we fail to leave room for God, we will end up living in an unrestricted stream of consciousness. We will be putting out fires rather than really accomplishing anything.

Don't be Edward I. Try!

There once was a Christian named Edward I. Try,
who looked very holy, no one could deny.
He went to church at least six times a week.
He served on committees and, when asked, he would speak.

LORDSHIP GENEROSITY

*He'd expound on the grace and the love of the Lord.
He'd take lots of notes on the Greek words he explored.
Edward I. Try exemplified speed,
as he tried to fulfill every ministry need.
For years he had taught and urged and greeted.
He spiritually washed and rinsed and repeated.
He silenced the gossips and soothed the old man
who refused to approve of the church building plan.
Edward was busy, gracious and careful.
He was thoughtful and smiling and apparently prayerful.
And at the right moments he seemed holy and solemn.
He was certainly a workhorse whatever you'd call him.
He had dreams of becoming a Christian sensation
and winning the acceptance of the entire congregation.
But after a while, his walk became weary.
His face appeared downcast, and his eyes became bleary.
He tried to mask the exhaustion and stress
that came from trying to fix every church mess.
Edward I. Try had lost all sense of hope
that he'd solve all the problems and be able to cope.
He cried out to God in a burst of rage:
I'm sick of all this. I'm leaving the stage!
I can't be a nursemaid to every hurt feeling.
I no longer find committees all that appealing.
I'm searching for peace, so give me a clue!
I'd rather sell pencils or play the kazoo,
than to be enslaved on this treadmill of work.
Because I don't feel like a saint; I feel more like a jerk!
After the tantrum, he stared at the ceiling,
realizing this prayer might seem unappealing.
But there in the silence of his '95 Ford,
he heard the gentle voice of his Lord.
At last, you've reached the end of your rope.*

I'm ecstatic that you abandoned your instinct to cope.
I never blessed your list of to-dos,
that gave you a case of the spiritual blues.
You see, now that you've admitted you don't have a clue,
You've finally become someone I can work through.
So, bring all burdens! Just cast them aside.
And watch what will happen when you choose to abide.

THE LORDSHIP PRAYER

The Christ follower who surrenders his or her schedule over to God will find so much more peace and personal contentment. Once again, it's transfer of ownership. We see this in the Lord's Prayer. This model prayer is a prayer of total surrender.

A common thread runs through every line of the Lord's Prayer that the Church has spoken together for centuries. We are articulating the power of releasing. We scan through the words and notice that the Lord's Prayer is radically different from the modern mantras of mortal yearning. Instead of coming to God and asking Him to change our circumstances, we encounter a releasing of ourselves into the gracious hand of the Father who knows exactly what we need before we ask.

Our Father in Heaven
I release my urge to play God with my circumstances.

Hallowed be thy Name.
I release any preconceived notion that am better than others in comparison to the reality of You.

Thy Kingdom come. Thy will be done on Earth as it is in Heaven.
I release my kingdom to embrace yours.

Give us this day our daily bread.
I release the desire to be a self-made provider.

And forgive us our debts as we forgive our debtors.
I release forgiveness to those who've wounded me, and I recognize and repent for the wounds I have caused to others and even to myself.

Lead us not into temptation.
I release my long-held belief that I am more powerful than my sins and addictions.

But deliver us from evil.
I release my appetite and familiarity with the evil one.

For thine is the Kingdom, the power and the glory forever, Amen.
I release my personal possessions, properties, fame, and strength to embrace all that is You.

When we release all these things, life becomes much simpler. Even when life is difficult (and it will be!), we find rest and release. If we let ourselves live inside the Lord's Prayer, we will find it to be life changing; it will be a daily blessing to us—even in the hard places. We will find that we can respond with thankfulness even our times of greatest difficulty!

- So, you are finding yourself in a lonely place? *Good.* The divine presence of God has been wanting to say something to you.
- So, you are financially crippled? *Good.* Perhaps you are here to discover how illogical reliance on money really is.
- So, you are exhausted? *Good.* It's time to rest. The rest Christ offers is the best you can have. Breathe. Drink deeply of His grace. Find rest for your soul.

- So, you are feeling tested? *Good.* God is setting you up for greater stewardship.
- So, you are grieving? *Good.* God is giving you a glimpse of the cross and His sorrow over lost humanity.
- So, you are angry? *Good.* As long as you are angry about the right things. If you are, knock over a few tables.
- So, you are empty? *Good.* This could be the perfect time for the Holy Spirit to rush into the void.
- So, you are confused? *Good.* There's no better time to cry out to God.
- So, you can't sleep? *Good.* Now is the time to be awake and listen.

Life becomes a celebration and a conversation with our Creator if we are willing to surrender everything over to Him. It's all about release. The other option is to keep striving when transformation and rest are waiting just beyond the tips of our fingers. It doesn't have to be that way if we would only surrender.

When we number, plan, and celebrate our days, life has the aroma of joy and holiness. It's different from the days we practice randomness, escapism, and confusion. So, what is the most important day in God's eyes? Perhaps it is today. What's right here right now is all we have to live in.

God holds the future and redeems all of yesterday. But today is closer to us. What an amazing concept today, right now, really is. Today—I hope you aren't planning a siege on your enemy. I hope you aren't judging the person in the room. I hope you aren't swallowed up in regret. I hope you aren't poisoning your time with trivial, toxic thoughts of your own wealth, vanity, or scheming revenge. I hope you are in the moment, for this moment fashions eternity.

> "When we number, plan, and celebrate our days, life has the aroma of joy and holiness."

Today is a gift that is moving forward faster than thoughts or plans. Today is where I am *right here* and *right now!* Today is an opportunity to change the little things. Today is closer. Tomorrow is a promise, and yesterday is an eternity from anything I could attain.

Today is most noble!

CHECK OUT THIS SHORT
EXPLAINER VIDEO BASED
ON THIS CHAPTER!

THE BALANCE OF YOUR TIME

**MARGINS MEANINGFUL
RESTED MAXIMIZED
PEOPLE CENTERED
RESPONSIVE DESTINED
PRIORITIZED PRESENT
RHYTHM-FOCUSED
JESUS IS LORD**

─────── OR ───────

**I AM LORD
WASTED EXHAUSTED
OVER-CAPACITY
MINDLESS UNPLANNED
URGENCY-FUELED
UNPRODUCTIVE
SCATTERED NEARSIGHTED**

LORDSHIP GENEROSITY

MOVEMENT 1
BALANCE OF YOUR TIME

- What amount of time did I spend in spiritual practices this past week? (Prayer, Bible Study and stillness)

- Did I have a true day of Sabbath where work was set aside to rest my mind, emotions, body, and spirit?

- What did I choose to watch for entertainment and information?

- What were the most eternal activities that I experienced?

- Who were the people I influenced this week?

MOVEMENT 2
THE EXPRESSION OF YOUR GIFTS

Now there are different gifts, but the same Spirit. There are different ministries, but the same Lord. And there are different activities, but the same God works all of them in each person. A manifestation of the Spirit is given to each person for the common good.
— 1 Corinthians 12:4-7

In the long history of the Universe, you are unique. But we can't all be special. Right? Actually, yes, we can. We are all specifically designed to fulfill our role with the gifts, talents, and perspective God has given us. Your uniqueness in the body of Christ speaks to the fact that God has a sovereign, divine purpose for every believer. This underscores the word of God to Jeremiah:

I chose you before I formed you in the womb;
I set you apart before you were born.
I appointed you a prophet to the nations.
— Jeremiah 1:5

Here's the deal. Your gifts are meant to be *regifted* to a hurting world. When we make Jesus lord, we generously leverage our own design for His purpose. The declaration made to Jeremiah in the above scripture speaks to the specific call God has on all of us. Granted, we aren't all called to be prophets, but God has appointed each of us to a specific task that no one else in this world is assigned to accomplish, like He did with Jeremiah. He formed you in the womb also. Your DNA, fingerprint, formative history, retina, and, yes, even your gut microbiome is unique. When God creates people, He's never making copies!

He's appointed some to be in the operating room, the cockpit, the soup kitchen, the board room, the courthouse, the cornfield, the pulpit, the youth worship service, the school, and in a million other unique places and circumstances. And it doesn't stop there. This providential calling is specific not just in role but also in place and time. As Mordechai said to Esther, *"Who knows, perhaps you have come to your royal position for such a time as this"* (Esth. 4:14).

> **"You have spiritual gifts."**

You were destined to be where you are and when you are! You have spiritual gifts. But perhaps more importantly, you are a spiritual gift. You are singularly unique. There are some things only you can teach me. There are certain ways in which you communicate the Gospel that only you can. Not because of your charisma, talent, and elocution… No. It is because of the unique story God tells simply and uniquely through you.

Your Story Changes You

Also, every experience that you've had up to this moment can be leveraged into your future task and calling. None of us ever come out of a relationship, a trauma, a move, an illness, a vocational role, or a heartbreak as the same person we were before the event or experience. We are constantly growing and changing. Sidenote: Although past experience often speaks into future reactions, we have to realize that since everyone is changing, we shouldn't completely become the predictor of what others will do or say in a present circumstance.

THE EXPRESSION OF YOUR GIFTS

One thing I know! In Christ, you have great potential. Yes, you. As Dwight L. Moody said, "The world has yet to see what God can do with someone who is fully consecrated to him." The tragic truth is that most Christians never fully surrender everything over to God so that they can be used completely and fully in His mission.

> **"When you steward your gifts well, you ultimately bring glory to God."**

Every Believer has Spiritual Gifts (Rom. 12:6-8).

Mark Twain said it best, "The two most important days in your life are the day you are born and the day you find out why." Your unique spiritual giftedness helps define the "why" of your being.

Jesus saved you for a purpose, and as a believer you received the stewardship responsibilities of your gifts and skills. When you steward your gifts well, you ultimately bring glory to God. Peter puts it this way:

Just as each one has received a gift, use it to serve others, as good stewards of the varied grace of God. If anyone speaks, let it be as one who speaks God's words; if anyone serves, let it be from the strength God provides, so that God may be glorified through Jesus Christ in everything. To him be the glory and the power forever and ever. Amen.
— 1 Peter 4:10-11

The Gift of Illumination and Revelation of Your Gifts

You know some of your gifts easily, while others require illumination. That's when we spend time with God and ask Him to reveal the gifts that He embedded in our souls. What are some ways you can determine your spiritual gift or gifts? Here are a few:

1. **Pray.** Ask the Father to help you be sensitive to His leading as He reveals your giftedness to you.
2. **Ask** someone close to you what they have observed in your skill set.
3. **Reflect** on your parents' gifts and skills.
4. **Test** the waters. Try it out. It won't take long for you to realize that "This isn't it" if indeed, this isn't it!
5. **Ask:** "What is my Christ-like impulse during a crisis or adversity?"

As you discover your spiritual gifts, it's important to activate and use them. This is every Christian's mandate. Peter reminds us: "Just as each one has received a gift, use it to serve others, as good stewards of the varied grace of God" (1 Pet. 4:10). We must ask ourselves, "Will we leverage our gifts and soar into God's destiny?

Sören Kierkegaard wrote a parable about this challenge:

THE PARABLE OF THE GEESE

"A certain flock of geese lived together in a barnyard with high walls around it. Because the corn was good and the barnyard was secure, these geese would never take a risk.

'One day a philosopher goose came among them. He was a very good philosopher and every week they listened quietly and attentively to his learned discourses. 'My fellow travelers on the way of life,' he would say, 'can you seriously imagine that this barnyard, with great high walls around it, is all there is to existence? I tell you, there is another and a greater world outside, a world of which we are only dimly aware. Our forefathers knew of this outside world. For did they not stretch their wings and fly across the trackless wastes of desert and ocean, of green valley and wooded hill? But alas, here we remain in this barnyard, our wings folded and tucked into our sides, as we are content to puddle in the mud, never lifting our eyes to the heavens which should be our home.'

'The geese thought this was very fine lecturing. 'How poetical,' they thought. 'How profoundly existential. What a flawless summary of the mystery of existence.' Often the philosopher spoke of the advantages of flight, calling on the geese to be what they were. After all, they had wings, he pointed out. What were wings for, but to fly with? Often, he reflected on the beauty and the wonder of life outside the barnyard, and the freedom of the skies.

'And every week the geese were uplifted, inspired, moved by the philosopher's message. They hung on his every word. They devoted hours, weeks, months to a thoroughgoing analysis and critical evaluation of his doctrines. They produced learned treatises on the ethical and spiritual implications of flight. All this they did. But one thing they never did. They did not fly! For the corn was good, and the barnyard was secure!"

You were born to fly, not to stay in the barn where the corn is good, and the barnyard is secure. To stay in the barn is not generous. Quite the contrary, it's rebellion against the lordship of Jesus.

Numerous books have been written to help people identify, understand, and use their spiritual gifts. If you are looking for a helpful guide, you may want to consider *Spiritual Gifts: A Practical Guide to How God Works Through You* (David Francis, 2003).

Also check out the spiritual gifts inventory in the back of this book.

Space is not going to allow us to do an in-depth study of all of the spiritual gifts; some, though, we want to spotlight.

1. Prophecy

The Greek word for the gift of prophecy is propheteia. It means the ability to receive a divinely inspired message and deliver it to others in the church.

This is how the apostle Paul spoke of prophecy: The person who prophesies speaks to people for their strengthening, encouragement and consolation. *"The person who speaks in a tongue builds himself up, but the one who prophesies builds up the church" (1 Cor. 14:4).*

Perhaps you know someone in your church who has the ability to speak a word of truth, exhortation, correction, or warning at just the right time. Such a person could be considered as having a gift of "speaking forth." They rise when others dare not speak. They are courageous and yet prudent to speak the truth with love and grace.

When most people think of a prophet, they think of someone who has the mystical, ethereal gift of foretelling the future like some of the Old Testament prophets did. Although that is a small segment of this larger group of people, the greater, more frequent habit of someone with the gift of prophecy is far more practical. They speak up with the right word, at the right time, in the right way. They speak out with a word from God. This was what most of the Old Testament prophets did, rather than foretelling future events.

Scripture shows that a prophet can be a man or a woman. It's hard to overlook this in the Old and New Testament. In the Old Testament we discover:

- Miriam (Exodus 15:20)
- Deborah (Judges 4:4)
- Huldah (2 Kings 22:14; 2 Chronicles 34:22)
- Noadiah (Nehemiah 6:14)
- And "the prophetess" (Isaiah 8:3)

Luke also wrote about Philip who was one of the seven deacons. He had four daughters who prophesied: *"The next day we left and came to Caesarea, where we entered the house of Philip the evangelist, who was one of the Seven, and stayed with him. This man had four virgin daughters who prophesied" (Acts 21:8-9).*

So, unlike some other gifts where gender roles are to be considered, (or in some circles, zealously debated!), the gift of prophecy has generous biblical support showing that a woman can prophesy.

THE EXPRESSION OF YOUR GIFTS

Here are a few other misconceptions concerning the gift of prophecy:

Misconception 1: Prophecy and preaching are the same thing.

Actually, they totally aren't the same! Preaching and prophecy are separated in the New Testament. Preaching is an exposition of the biblical text. Prophecy is speaking forth a word that the Lord has given for the body. Prophecy will not always begin with a biblical text, but it will NEVER disagree with what God has revealed in His Word.

Misconception 2: Prophecy is all about predicting the future.

Prophecy may portend future events, but someone who has the gift of prophecy is not psychic. He or she doesn't hold the secret timing of future events. Instead, think of the person with the gift of prophecy as someone who connects with God is such a way as to discern matters of the heart and speak God's message into the lives of individuals or into the local body of Christ. Perhaps your spouse has this gift. After a meeting with a person that both of you don't know very well, your spouse may say that something is amiss. He or she is wary about something that was said, an attitude, or an action. Sometimes this is prophecy. Other times this feeling is more like a holy hunch.

> "Think of the person with the gift of prophecy as someone who connects with God is such a way as to discern matters of the heart and speak God's message into the lives of individuals or into the local body of Christ."

Misconception 3: Prophets are leaders in the church.

There is no biblical proof that having the gift of prophecy grants someone with a set position in the church or that a prophet would have authority over a certain area of a church. Prophets don't always make the best leaders. Why? Many times, the prophet's words can create pain or offense. Thus, we often see the gift of prophecy accompanied by a healthy dose of courage. And again, they're not always suited to be leaders.

2. Serving

We are all called to serve; the Holy Spirit, though, seems to endow people with this amazing gift in an extraordinary measure. Perhaps when you think of someone with the gift of service, you imagine that this person can't do anything else of greater importance in the body. That's not the case! The gift of service should be celebrated as one of the most impactful gifts in the body.

The people with the gift of service are happy to work in areas far from the spotlight. They are the ones that meet the needs of hurting people; find solutions to predicaments and problems; and are quick to pick up a broom, a wrench, or the keys to the church van to do what Jesus would do. *"Next, he poured water into a basin and began to wash the disciples' feet and to dry them with the towel tied around him"* (John 13:5).

Obviously, Jesus personified the gift of service in human form. He said of Himself, *"For even the Son of Man did not come to be served, but to serve, and to give his life as a ransom for many"* (Mark 10:45).

As mentioned above, all Christians are called to serve. Still there are some whose servant-hearted way of life is supernaturally expressed. The one who has a gift of serving seems to see needs others may not; they then lean into that need as an expression of their faith. Paul urged the church at Philippi to follow after Jesus through humble service, which is expressed in looking after the interests of others:

If, then, there is any encouragement in Christ, if any consolation of love, if any fellowship with the Spirit, if any affection and mercy, make my joy complete by thinking the same way, having the same love, united in spirit, intent on one purpose. Do nothing out of selfish ambition or conceit, but

in humility consider others as more important than yourselves. Everyone should look not to his own interests, but rather to the interests of others.
— *Philippians 2:1-4*

When we serve, we are generously radiating the lordship of Jesus! How did He live? As mentioned before, He came to serve. One of the most abbreviated descriptions of Jesus's work came from Simon Peter. He stated that under the power of the Holy Spirit, *"He [Jesus] went about doing good" (Acts 10:38)*. What a simple but profound declaration!

From the beginning, Jesus came to make service His mode of operation. This great mystery never gets old. The one who created it all stooped into this messed-up world to serve. And now He's inviting us to be just as generous in serving as He was. It's called Lordship Generosity.

3. Teaching

The gift of teaching is the specific ability of a believer to impart spiritual truth that ultimately transforms the lives of other people. We've all been influenced by teachers who could take the mystery and marvel of Scripture and communicate it in a way that transforms people. The teacher's goal isn't to create believers who know all the trivial details and intellectual theories of the Bible. The spiritual teacher is someone who takes God's Word and serves God by motivating change in the lives of believers. It's not merely the ability of teachers that makes it a gift; it's the growth that happens under their leadership.

It's also fascinating that God gives some the gift of teaching adults, while others are given the gift of teaching youth, children, or preschoolers. God gives each teacher one or more expressions of the gift. Some are:

Experiential: "Let's learn by doing something together."
Conversational: "Let's dialogue about this part of the Bible. I have a few questions. Let's discuss them. I have some truths to share, but I want to hear your thoughts."
Visual: "Let me graph out how this spiritual process works."
Musical: "This song beautifully describes what I'm trying to say."
Humor: "That reminds me of a funny story."
Emotional: "I want you to feel what I'm feeling."

Keep in mind that an effective teacher rarely uses only one instructional expression. Most great teachers work with a mix of techniques and styles. But oftentimes God supernaturally gifts a teacher to use one of these specific teaching expressions or methods extraordinarily. You know when you see a teacher who could be doing almost anything else but chooses to teach. They make the most of this opportunity. That's generosity. Lordship Generosity.

> "The spiritual teacher is someone who takes God's Word and serves God by motivating change in the lives of believers."

4. Exhortation

The gift of exhortation, also known as the gift of encouragement, is the God-given art of inspiring and motivating others. People with this gift have a natural talent to do three things:

- Encourage
- Comfort
- Guide

People with this gift often have a deep empathy for others. They understand people's needs and struggles and offer words of support and inspiration to uplift and strengthen others.

Those with the gift of exhortation are effective communicators who excel in verbal encouragement. They have a way with words and can speak truth with love, by edifying and building up those who hear. These encouragers often find joy in helping others discover their potential, urging them to persevere, and spurring them on to live a life of faith and purpose.

The gift of exhortation is not limited to public speaking or formal ministry roles. It can manifest in various contexts, such as one-on-one conversations, small group settings, teaching, counseling, mentoring, or even writing. People with this gift are often sought after for their wisdom, guidance, and ability to provide timely and uplifting words.

The ultimate goal of encouragement is to bring God glory by strengthening other believers. The focus of the encourager is always others. In a self-centered world, this gift of encouragement is both rare and powerful!

The Bible contains several examples of encouragers:

Barnabas: Barnabas, whose name means "Son of Encouragement," is a prominent figure in the New Testament. We first read of Barnabas in Acts 4:36-37, where he sold a field and donated the proceeds to the early Christian community. Barnabas had a well-deserved reputation for generosity and encouragement towards others, especially Paul (formerly known as Saul). He vouched for Paul's conversion and helped him integrate into the Christian community, despite initial skepticism from others (Acts 9:26-28). Barnabas played a significant role in encouraging and supporting Paul throughout his ministry.

Paul: The apostle Paul himself was not only a recipient of encouragement but also a great source of encouragement to others. Through his letters and personal interactions, Paul encouraged various individuals and communities in their faith. He often expressed his love, care, concern, and prayers for them. He provided spiritual guidance and urged them to persevere in their commitment to Christ.

Epaphroditus: The Book of Philippians mentions Epaphroditus as a fellow worker and companion of Paul. When the Philippian church sent him to provide support and encouragement to Paul during his imprisonment, Epaphroditus became seriously ill. When he recovered, Paul commended him for his dedication and encouraged the Philippian believers to receive him with joy and honor (Phil. 2:25-30).

> **"The focus of the encourager is always others."**

Priscilla and Aquila: Priscilla and Aquila were a married couple who played a vital role in the early Christian community. They provided encouragement and instruction to Apollos, a gifted speaker who needed further understanding of the Gospel (Acts 18:24-26). Priscilla and Aquila opened their home to fellow believers, hosted gatherings, and supported the growth of the early church.

Each of these biblical characters are models of people who were generous in encouragement and reflected Who was the lord of their lives. It's not hard to be encouraging, but it is life-changing.

When we encourage people,

We build people up.
Therefore encourage one another and build each other up as you are already doing (1 Thess. 5:11).

We help them have courage.
Haven't I commanded you: be strong and courageous? Do not be afraid or discouraged, for the Lord your God is with you wherever you go (Josh. 1:9).

We do it daily.
But encourage each other daily, while it is still called today, so that none of you is hardened by sin's deception (Heb. 3:13).

We help them with their struggles.
Carry one another's burdens; in this way you will fulfill the law of Christ (Gal. 6:2).

We watch over people.
And let us consider one another in order to provoke love and good works (Heb. 10:24).

5. Giving

Just as all believers are to be encouragers, we are all called to give. Some Christians, though, have the extraordinary gift of overflowing generosity. These believers are constantly looking for opportunities to invest in ministry and inspire us all to give.

The Bible offers instructions about how believers are to give—both in the attitude and actions a giver is to have. Writing to believers living in Corinth, Paul spoke of the giver's attitude: *"Each person should do as he has decided in his heart—not reluctantly or out of compulsion, since God loves a cheerful giver"* (2 Cor. 9:7). The Greek word for "cheerful" is *hilaros*, from which we get the word "hilarious." The face of this type of giver radiates satisfaction and joy rather than fear and hesitancy.

Concerning action, Paul instructed: *"On the first day of the week, each of you is to set something aside and save in keeping with how he is prospering"* (1 Cor.16:2). This giving does not happen by accident; it is planned: *"on the first day of the week."* The old adage applies to giving to the Lord's work: Failing to plan is planning to fail. This giving is also proportionate, *"in keeping with how he is prospering."* What one person gives does not dictate what someone else gives. We are reminded of Jesus taking note of the widow who gave the two mites. Comparing her to those who gave out of their abundance, Jesus said, *"she out of her poverty has put in all she had to live on"* (Luke 21:4).

Those who have the spiritual gift of giving will have already met these attitudes and actions—but then they go further. Led by the Holy Spirit, they have an inner compulsion to give beyond what others might expect. Mentioned above, Barnabas is an example of someone who gave extravagantly. He *"sold a field he owned, brought the money, and laid it at the apostles' feet"* (Acts 4:37).

Three principles come into play with this type of giving.

- First, *others may not understand it and might even be critical.* Recall the disciples' reaction when a woman anointed Jesus with expensive perfume: *"When the disciples saw it, they were indignant. 'Why this waste?' they asked. 'This might have been sold for a great deal and given to the poor'"* (Matt. 26:8-9, emphasis added). The disciples (not just Judas) did not understand someone giving with such reckless abandon. Family and friends—even other believers—may not comprehend such lavish giving.

- Second, *those with the spiritual gift of giving do not share extravagantly in order to garner attention or the praise of others.* They do so because of the prompting of the Holy Spirit. They have found what Jesus said was true: *"It is more blessed to give than to receive"* (Acts 20:35). In giving, they find themselves to be blessed in a way that is spiritually satisfying.

I (GB) have a friend who has the spiritual gift of giving. One of the ways he exercises this gift is to support pastors who are just entering the ministry. Often these guys are still in seminary and serving in smaller churches with limited resources. My friend helps supplement the pastor's salary by sending a regular cash gift that anonymously shows up in the mail or by helping pay for his seminary tuition. Using his spiritual gift of giving, he practices Lordship Generosity.

- Third, *people who have the spiritual gift of giving do not see it as a means of manipulating God to give them more.* They do not give in order to get; instead, they understand that God gives to them so that they can give to others. Those with this gift intend to serve as a conduit through which God blesses other people and ministries.

Some TV evangelists appeal to people's greed and try to manipulate them to support them and their ministries with the promise that "If you will give to me, God will give to you." They highlight the verse that says, *"The person who sows sparingly will also reap sparingly, and the person who sows generously will also reap generously"* (2 Cor. 9:6). And a favorite verse often highlighted is Jesus's promise to His disciples, *"there is no one who has left house or brothers or sisters or mother or father or children or fields for my sake and for the sake of the gospel, who will not receive a hundred times more."* The pinch is that these TV evangelists often fail to finish the verse, which continues, *". . . now at this time — houses, brothers and sisters, mothers and children, and fields, with persecutions — and eternal life in the age to come"* (Mark 10:29-30, emphasis added).

> **"Led by the Holy Spirit, they have an inner compulsion to give beyond what others might expect."**

6. Leadership

Leadership guru, Dr. John Maxwell, is famous for saying, "Everything rises or falls on leadership." This maxim is proven true over and again in any organization — whether in a company, school, governmental entity, family, or church. A lack of effective leadership leads to discouragement, confusion, frustration, and eventually anger and defeat.

Although some people seem to be "natural-born leaders," for those who aren't, countless books have been written to help develop leadership skills. One prolific author was the late Peter Drucker. His influence on leadership and management development in the business world can hardly be overstated. Drucker defined leadership as "the lifting of a man's vision to higher sights, the raising of a man's performance to a higher standard, the building of a man's personality beyond its normal limitations."[2]

How, though, does the spiritual gift of leadership differ from what we find in secular society? The difference comes mainly in the way the person with the gift intends to use it. He or she will have a different motivation and intended goal.

As mentioned above, Simon Peter said of spiritual gifts: *"Just as each one has received a gift, use it to serve others, as good stewards of the varied grace of God. . . . so that God may be glorified through Jesus Christ in everything. To him be the glory and the power forever and ever"* (1 Pet. 4:10-11). The motivation behind implementing the spiritual gift of leadership will ultimately be to bring glory to God. It is not about the company, the budget, the bottom line, or even the project itself. The purpose is that *"God may be glorified through Jesus Christ."*

In writing to believers living in Rome, Paul said that those with this gift are to lead *"with diligence"* (Rom. 12:8). This description almost seems redundant; one can hardly imagine an effective leader who is lazy, timid, or cowardly. Yet, Paul underscored this essential trait.

One of the great biblical examples of a diligent leader is Nehemiah. After having lived as an exile, he returned to Jerusalem and inspected the city walls, which the Babylonians destroyed in 586 BC. After seeing the walls' condition, he came up with a plan, conveyed his vision, and enlisted workers. He made assignments, secured materials, addressed the opposition, and gave leadership

THE EXPRESSION OF YOUR GIFTS

to the work. Because of Nehemiah's effective leadership, the protective wall around Jerusalem was completed in just 52 days, using an all-volunteer labor force.

Several facets are included in the spiritual gift of leadership — and we see these in Nehemiah. Persons with this gift understand God's purpose, set goals that relate to fulfilling that purpose, and share those goals in a way that motivates people to get involved voluntarily in the task. All of this they do to the glory of God. Thus, the gift has to do with vision casting, planning, and moving the project or task toward completion.

People with this spiritual gift are compelled to find a way to put it to use — whether in a religious or secular setting. In secular settings, those with the spiritual gift of leadership can serve as a light in the darkness, helping give God-honoring direction to a company or organization. In church and ministry settings, they are the vision casters who help God's people collaboratively accomplish His work for His glory.

> "A lack of effective leadership leads to discouragement, confusion, frustration, and eventually anger and defeat."

Some Surprising Things about Leadership:

- **Leadership is not getting everyone to agree on everything.**

Unity is primary to the church. Paul uses lots of ink communicating the power of unity and the tragedy of schisms within the church. But if you ever get to the point where you feel you've got to get unanimous votes, you'll set yourself up for failure, disappointment, and unnecessary obsessing. There is power in uniting leaders when they disagree, while also respecting those whose opinions vary even in the nuances of a ministry strategy. The most successful leaders are the ones who might disagree behind closed doors but choose to galvanize the mission by presenting a united front to the church after a decision is made. That is leadership and, yes, it is surprising, crazy-talk leadership.

- **Leadership requires fear and hate.**

When we think of leadership, we think of the word courageous. But inherent in every leader, there must also be fear and hate. We must fear many things! We must fear leading alone. We need each other. The warmest words a pastor will ever hear during conflict is, "I've got your back." We must fear complacency, sin, temptation, impurity, and missing God in the mission.

> "The most successful leaders are the ones who might disagree behind closed doors but choose to galvanize the mission by presenting a united front"

We must also hate a few things. We must hate gossip, lies, shadow missions, and a score of other things that jeopardize our mission and the church. Leaders must hate with great skill the things we should hate.

Think about it. We serve a God who hates. In Proverbs, the Bible tells us of this Holy God who hates seven things:

Arrogant Eyes,
A Lying Tongue,
Hands That Shed Innocent Blood,
A Heart That Plots Wicked Schemes,
Feet Eager to Run to Evil,
A Lying Witness Who Gives False Testimony,
And One Who Stirs Up Trouble Among Brothers.
– Proverbs 6:16-19

Be a godly leader and hate the right stuff.

- **Leadership is as much about the journey as it is about getting from here to there.**

Jesus was a traveling leader who had a busy three-year tour of the Middle East on foot, boats, and donkey. But if you read the Gospels, the destinations usually took a back seat to what happened along the way. Demons, storms, dead guys, Romans, tax collectors, roadside meals, wave walking.... Wow! There was a lot to see along the journey.

As Forrest Gump said: "Now, it used to be, I ran to get where I was goin'. I never thought it would take me anywhere." Our greatest moments in leadership often occur along the way and not simply at the destination.

- **Leadership is not about knowing what should be done.**

There are lots of people who KNOW what should be done, but churches are often hamstrung because nobody is DOING what should be done. Mental gymnastics and philosophical leadership should be left to the Pharisees. We are called to be disciples. The very word connotes action.

- **Leadership is about failing often.**

Yes, this seems very ironic. But if your team is counting on home runs every time they try to lead people, then frustration will soon follow. In the same breath, we must do everything we can to achieve our goals. It's true: God doesn't ask us to be successful; He asks us to be faithful. Results are a God thing, not an "us" thing. And sometimes the only way we get it right is by getting it wrong and correcting course.

- **Leadership is not a personality type.**

Leaders come in all styles, colors, shapes, and shoe-sizes. Some of the greatest leaders are introverts. They are listeners and when they speak, people listen. Do you know what kind of leaders you need on the team? Quiet leaders who listen and contemplate. Loud leaders who aren't afraid of a microphone. Skilled leaders who know how to fix a septic tank or a computer. Funny leaders who provide joy and excitement. (I think you know where I'm going with this.)

We need writers, huggers, van drivers, poets, carpenters, negotiators, truth tellers, and finger-in-your-chest leaders. There is a place at the leadership table for them all.

7. Mercy

The life and work of Florence Nightingale were truly remarkable. She helped establish effective nursing procedures for the wounded who had been sent to field hospitals in the mid-1800s. Her work led to her being called an "Angel of Mercy." One of the details she noticed in her work was that the patients whom the doctors saw earlier in the morning seemed to improve more quickly. After consideration, she came to the conclusion that it was because the doctors' clothes, medical utensils, and hands were clean when they first started in the morning—but they became increasingly soiled as the day went on. She implemented a policy of having her nurses wash their hands and change their aprons before visiting each patient. Although it was a radical idea at the time and was met by strong resistance and even hostility, her procedures eventually became standard care. As a result, health conditions began to improve dramatically.

The spiritual gift of mercy always carries with it the idea of demonstrating compassion and help for the hurting and needy. It is a special gift that God gives to some people to deliver His care, kind-heartedness, love, healing, and hope to those who are, as the old hymn says, "weak and wounded, sick and sore."

Some have differentiated between compassion and mercy. They argue that compassion is rooted in having feelings of pity or empathy for other people and their life situations. Mercy, in contrast, is putting action to one's feelings of compassion. The action can be to forgive someone or to assist with what is causing them hurt.

As Jesus was leaving Jericho, blind Bartimaeus cried out, *"Jesus, Son of David, have mercy on me!" (Mark 10:47)*. Jesus certainly felt compassion for Bartimaeus, but He responded with mercy and healed his blindness. Similarly, in His story of the "good Samaritan," Jesus explained that the neighbor to the injured man was *"the one who showed mercy to him" (Luke 10:37)*. Again, mercy is compassion put into action.

> "There are lots of people who KNOW what should be done, but churches are often hamstrung because nobody is DOING what should be done."

In His Sermon on the Mount, Jesus declared, *"Blessed are the pure in heart, for they will see God" (Matt. 5:8)*. Jesus expects all of His disciples to show mercy and compassion to others. Those with this gift, though, show mercy in doses that are greater than one normally finds in others. They offer mercy—not by the teaspoon but by dump-truck loads.

Paul stated that those with the gift of mercy put it to use *"with cheerfulness" (Rom. 12:8)*. Thus, the gift makes itself known in both the abundance of the tender-hearted help and the positive attitude with which it is delivered.

It's important to note that there's no one all-inclusive gift list in the Bible. They are described in the New Testament, primarily in 1 Corinthians 12, Romans 12, and Ephesians 4. First Peter 4 also mentions spiritual gifts. Some of the gifts are natural talents and others are supernatural; what we need to keep in mind is that all gifts should be cultivated and used for God's glory. God empowers you in everything He has given you. It's easy for us to forget that *"you can do nothing without me (Jesus)" (John 15:5).*

You've heard it said of an organization, "That place is a well-oiled machine." Other organizations feel large, daunting, and all consuming. We think of them as a beast to be tamed and harnessed. No doubt you've heard people say about their jobs, "It's time to feed the beast."

The Body of Christ is not a machine or a beast. It's a body, a living organism; and we all have a role. Your role is unique. In the history of mankind no one has ever been you! God has a specific purpose for you; and He created you with a specific set of inherent skills, gifts, genes, and yes, even defects to accomplish His purpose and live the life you've been created to live within the body of Christ and in the specific place and time God placed you.

Ask for Spiritual Gifts. One more note about spiritual gifts: We need to constantly ask God for spiritual gifts. We know that God is a good Father who loves to give His children gifts. There are gifts that you have cultivated over time.

We grow in our spiritual gifts. And the best way to do that is to practice what God has given you. Carve out time to reflect, pray, and meditate on your purpose and mission. Ask God to make you mindful of your purpose. As Mordecai said to Esther: *"Who knows, perhaps you have come to your royal position for such a time as this" (Esth. 4:14).* Wouldn't it be a tragedy to reach the end of your busy life only to realize that you never stopped to listen and be mindful about your ultimate purpose and giftings?

> **"It's important to note that there's no one all-inclusive gift list in the Bible."**

Journal your days. We'd do well to follow the instruction God gave to Habakkuk:

The LORD answered me: Write down this vision; clearly inscribe it

on tablets so one may easily read it. For the vision is yet for the appointed time; it testifies about the end and will not lie. Though it delays, wait for it, since it will certainly come and not be late.
— Hab 2:2-3

Be Patient. Developing spiritual gifts is a gradual process. Be open to the journey, and don't rush or force the process. Patience and persistence are key.

Listen to your friends. Often, they'll be able to give you feedback about what your spiritual gifts are and what they are not.

Do something new. The best way to learn something new is to do something new. Take the risk of getting outside of your comfort zone:

- Substitute for a Children's Sunday School teacher.
- Pick up a guitar.
- Ride shotgun with your pastor on a hospital visit.
- Go to a recovery group.
- Chaperone a student event.
- Sign up for a short-term mission trip.
- Get trained and serve in Disaster Relief.

As mentioned, these are just some of the spiritual gifts we find at work in the church. Each gift you possess is meant to be discovered, cultivated, and practiced. We use these gifts to bless the church and reach the spiritually lost. They are supernatural! Why? Because we are vessels of God's glory.

An amazing thing about spiritual gifts is that they come through us and not from us. When we realize where our gifts come from, the pressure to be successful or accepted diminishes. You can live out your gifts without worrying about the trap of success and performance. So, it's OK if we fail. If we speak the truth and no one accepts it. If we run through the fire and we are left without a friend. If we are far from the applause of our peers and our families—if no one sees a thing we do for Christ, it doesn't matter. You are living for the Audience of One. We don't have to obsess over how we look, what we accomplish, or where we are sent. It all goes back to Jesus.

> **"You can live out your gifts without worrying about the trap of success and performance."**

The only thing that matters at the end of the race is what we contain and into whose arms we fall when we gasp our last breath and cross the finish line. As long as we carry around in our body the death of Jesus, so that the life of Jesus may also be revealed in our body, we are infinitely more than what we ever could be on our own. This is a life-changing lesson, one that Paul taught the believers living in Corinth. *"Now we have this treasure in clay jars, so that this extraordinary power may be from God and not from us"* (2 Cor. 4:7).

We're all just vessels. It's not who we are that makes the work and our gifts glorious. It's Jesus. Always Jesus.

CHECK OUT THIS SHORT
EXPLAINER VIDEO BASED
ON THIS CHAPTER!

ETERNAL PURPOSEFUL
JOYFULLY SHARED FOCUSED
ACTIVE TRANSCENDENT
SUPERNATURAL SACRIFICIAL

JESUS IS LORD

— OR —

I AM LORD

UNREALIZED FLESH-DRIVEN
WEAK DORMANT
POWERLESS DOUBTFUL
EGOCENTRIC THREATENED

LORDSHIP GENEROSITY

MOVEMENT 2
THE EXPRESSION OF YOUR GIFTS

- How did I express my spiritual gifts this week?

- What activities did I participate in that allowed me to grow in my spiritual gifts?

- What positive outcomes did I witness from the expression of spiritual gifts?

- What did I learn about how God created me this week?

- Who did I encourage when I witnessed someone utilizing their gifts?

MOVEMENT 3
THE STEWARDSHIP OF YOUR FINANCES

People see money as an asset. God views money quite differently. He sees it as a barometer. How we manage our money reflects our values, motives, and even our faith. When Jesus wanted to move people towards Lordship, He would sometimes challenge them in the realm of money and possessions. We see this clearly in His encounter with a man we call "the rich young ruler."

As he was setting out on a journey, a man ran up, knelt down before him, and asked him, "Good teacher, what must I do to inherit eternal life?"

"Why do you call me good?" Jesus asked him. "No one is good except God alone. You know the commandments: Do not murder; do not commit adultery; do not steal; do not bear false witness; do not defraud; honor your father and mother."

He said to him, "Teacher, I have kept all these from my youth."

Looking at him, Jesus loved him and said to him, "You lack one thing: Go, sell all you have and give to the poor, and you will have treasure in Heaven. Then come, follow me." But he was dismayed by this demand, and he went away grieving, because he had many possessions.
— Mark 10:17-22

The lesson for this man wasn't really about money; it was about Lordship! Jesus used money as a test of this man's commitment to Him. In the same way, He wants to teach us to be willing to transfer the ownership of everything we have to Him. The great thing about Jesus is that He can be trusted. We trust him with our finances because ultimately, it's all His to begin with.

Tithing is more than a mere financial transaction; it's our opportunity to say to God, "I trust You. It all belongs to You anyway, and I choose to rely on Your ability to provide." It's practical and supernatural. It reflects the understanding that every area of life — including finances — should be subject to God's Lordship. We take God at his word when He promised that He's more than enough!

"Bring the whole tenth into the storehouse so that there may be food in my house. Test me in this way," says the LORD of Armies, "See if I will not open the floodgates of heaven and pour a blessing for you without measure"
— Mal. 3:10

We view tithing as an opportunity to experience God's faithfulness and blessings in our lives.

Impact on the Church Community

Tithing is God's way of challenging our faith and of supporting the local church. It's an ancient test of lordship and generosity that pays huge spiritual dividends. When we tithe, we are funding the mission of our church, and our church is helping fund missionaries and ministries around the world through the Cooperative Program.

Our tithe is a statement of unity and shared purpose. By contributing sacrificially, believers demonstrate their commitment to their church's vision and mission. This shared commitment strengthens the bonds of fellowship and encourages collaboration among believers, which helps create and cultivate a thriving and vibrant church community.

Challenges and Considerations

From the onset, we recognize that tithing presents its own set of unique challenges and considerations. Some individuals may struggle with the idea of giving a tenth of their income, particularly in the face of financial hardships or uncertainties. Churches must approach tithing with sensitivity, emphasizing the principle of cheerful giving and of providing support for those facing financial difficulties.

So, your pastor preaches on giving? Thank him. A pastor who invites members to tithe is inviting them into a life-changing, soul-transforming experience that affects every area of their lives. In truth, it's unfair to you if your pastor is not teaching you about this principle that has changed history in ways we'll never completely know until we get to Heaven!

Here's the short list of reasons you should be giving a tithe (10 percent of your income) to your local church:

It's worship. Whether you're in a church with electric guitars or a pipe organ, everybody should have an opportunity to give because from Genesis to Revelation, the Bible teaches that giving is an act of worship. Think about what you are doing when you illogically say goodbye to a large slice of your income that you could be using somewhere else and doing something else with it. You are saying, "Lord, above everything, I believe in You. It all belongs to You! My giving this money to my church is a symbol of my complete belief, trust, and dependence on You to be my everything."

Imagine you were there with Jesus when a beloved follower, Mary, enters the room carrying a year's salary in the form of a rare and exquisite ointment ornately encased. The assembly watches in disbelief. The vessel is broken, and the aroma of worship fills the room. She had wearied of logic, caution, safety, investments, and prudence. This is not the time for such things. This is a time for over-the-top, reckless, radical, unstoppable, extreme, extravagant WORSHIP.

Her only desire is Jesus. Her desire is fulfilled. This moment and encounter led her to squander her riches on the head and feet of the soon-scarred Savior. Her hands drip with the oil of adoration. In one moment, one woman worships Him more than most will in a lifetime. This is not just a tithe, as the Pharisee would desire. This is not a special missions offering, as the disciples would desire. This is not a retribution, penalty, or fine as the legalists would demand for her sin. This is overwhelming. This is reckless abandon. This is worship. This is bliss. This is EVERYTHING she had.

> "This is overwhelming. This is reckless abandon. This is worship This is bliss. This is EVERYTHING she had."

It's a promise. Here's the deal. The Lord says: If you'll be faithful in this area of obedience, I promise you that I'll take care of everything you're going to need. Trust me in this. You cannot out-give me" See Luke 6:38:

"Give, and it will be given to you; a good measure – pressed down, shaken together, and running over – will be poured into your lap. For with the measure you use, it will be measured back to you."

Corrie ten Boom and her sister were both imprisoned at the Ravensbruck concentration camp for hiding their Jewish friends from Hitler's brutal reign. Betsie fell ill along with 25 other inmates. Corrie had one little bottle of liquid vitamins. She had to decide if she would share or just take care of her sister. Betsie insisted they share, believing God would provide. Amazingly, every time she tipped the bottle another drop would come out. Finally, a guard smuggled another bottle. They were thrilled! Corrie returned to the miracle bottle and shook it. Nothing came out. God provided everything they needed, just in time! Corrie famously penned these words: "Faith sees the invisible, believes the unbelievable, and receives the impossible."

It's a teacher. If you want to teach your kids the best way to handle money and to be financially responsible, teach them about the tithe. Tithing teaches us how to avoid the virus of materialism and learn the bliss of generosity. For the family, tithing is an adventure in generosity. It's perhaps the greatest lesson your kids can learn in the brief time they are under your roof.

When we talk to our children about generosity as a core value, we can do it in five different ways:

1. We can open our Bible with them. We can use stories and teachings from the Bible to emphasize the value of generosity.

2. We can show them how we do it. Parents and other adults in the Christian community model generosity through their actions. Children learn by observing how adults give their time, resources, and care to others in need.

3. We can teach them the difference between needs and wants. This helps children understand the importance of prioritizing giving to others, even when it means sacrificing some personal desires.

4. We can make it a project. Parents can guide their children to give generously by setting generosity goals for projects, like the Lottie Moon Christmas Offering, or by adopting a child through Compassion International.

5. We can show them the needs all around us through participating together with service projects such as volunteering at homeless shelters, nursing homes, and mission trips.

It's a blessing. A young adult tried to convince his 86-year-old grandfather that he really didn't need to worry about tithing because he wasn't really making any money and was living on very little. The grandfather replied, "Why would I want to give up doing the one thing that makes my life have meaning and purpose?" He knew that once you begin the journey of generosity and tithing, God will carry you through and enrich your life far beyond any money that you hold on to. As the apostle Paul said to the Ephesian elders: *"In every way I've shown you that it is necessary to help the weak by laboring like this and to remember the words of the Lord Jesus, because he said, 'It is more blessed to give than to receive'"* (Acts 20:35).

It's a provision. When you tithe, you're taking care of the facilities of your church, its ministries, the minster(s), and their families. As mentioned earlier, if your church gives through the Cooperative Program, you are a solution to ministries and missions all over the world. Through the Cooperative Program, your church becomes a part of a myriad of missions and ministries including:
- Funding over 3,700 international missionaries all over the world.
- Providing funds for seminary students.
- Evangelizing students on college campuses by providing Baptist Collegiate Ministries.
- Funding Baptist Children's Homes.
- Fueling Compassion Ministries.
- Providing resources for Disaster Relief.
- And more!

It's a test. Throughout Scripture, God is continually testing those who follow Him. Across the pages, we see men and women struggling with a God who dares them to trust Him a little more every day. But in one area of our lives, God actually invites us to test Him. It is in this thing called the tithe. He says, "Test me! I dare you! I will come through. (see Mal. 3:10)

It's also a test for you as a follower. God knows that money is a strong and effective indicator of the condition of your heart. We see a powerful example of lordship in the life of an inventor and businessman who gained an international reputation for generosity and integrity.

Robert Gilmour LeTourneau (or R.G., as he was called) was born in Vermont in 1888. Dropping out of school in the sixth grade, he took correspondence courses to learn mechanics and engineering. He had his first job at the age of 14, working in an iron foundry. He worked several jobs in the next few years but developed a love for machinery.

He worked in a Navy shipyard in World War I. Returning home afterward and having no other employment options, he was hired to level some land for a wealthy rancher. He loved it! In the years that followed he turned this passion into a business. R.G. eventually developed amazing innovations in earth-moving equipment. His business continued to grow, even during the Great Depression. It recorded a profit of $52,000 in 1932 to over $1.4 million profit in 1938. In today's dollars (2023), that meant he grew his business from $1.1 million to $31.2 million during the Depression.

> "Why would I want to give up doing the one thing that makes my life have meaning and purpose?"

Sensing a call to ministry, he talked to his pastor. Wisely, his pastor assured him that God could use Christian businessmen for His glory as much as those who serve in traditional ministry roles. R.G. stayed the course.

God blessed his work and business. His company became the largest earth-moving machinery manufacturer in the world at the time. In 1935, his wife suggested they reverse their giving. Rather than give a tithe of 10%, the two agreed to give 90% to the Lord's work and to live off 10%. They did this based on one of John Wesley's oft-quoted sayings, "It's not how much money I will give to God, but how much of God's money will I keep for myself."

LeTourneau sponsored mission work in South America and Africa and founded LeTourneau Technical Institute (now

LeTourneau University) in Longview, Texas. In his lifetime, he was considered one of the greatest Christian businessmen of all time. His was an amazing life and testimony to Lordship Generosity.

It's an investment. So much of the resources we spend are slippery. They go for things that will be broken, consumed, experienced, expired, outdated, and eventually cast aside. But when we put our money in the plate, we are investing in something that has unlimited impact. Lives will be touched. Hearts changed. The hungry will be fed and the naked clothed. Thus, the investment of the tithe is sure.

The investment through your tithe is placing your finances in the hands of the greatest resource manager ever. We can trust His hands with the returns and the dividends of our generosity!

It's eternal. And the reason it is sure is that it is eternal. None of us will bring our cars, our homes, our 401ks, our boats, our jewels, or our food into Heaven. Our tithe though, is a different story altogether. We are investing in a kingdom that is built to last. And last FOREVER. The calculations of compounding interest over 30 years are quite impressive to most people. Can you get your brain around compounded interest over 30,000 years? The lives that are saved, the movements that are started, the resources that are provided—these have eternal impact. The greatest investment we can make is an investment in eternity!

> **"The investment through your tithe is placing your finances in the hands of the greatest resource manager ever."**

It's a miracle. When you open yourself up to giving through the tithe, you get a glimpse into the supernatural. Ask the tither if supernatural provision has ever happened in their years of giving, and inevitably the answer is, "Yes." For some reason, God rewards the tither with a glimpse of the supernatural.

There's an old Pre-Reformation story that's worth telling when Thomas Aquinas met Pope Innocent II. He found the Pope counting a pile of money. The Pope bragged, "Thomas, the church can no longer say, 'Silver and gold have I none.'" Aquinas replied, "Holy father, but neither can she now say, 'In the Name of Jesus, Arise, take up thy bed, and walk.'"

Setting aside all the theological chasms inherit in the underpinnings of that era, there's some truth in that old tale. Sometimes when we are living in a world of ease, comfort, and self-sufficiency, we miss the miraculous rhythm of sole-dependency upon God.

It's tax-deductible. Sorry, but the accountant in me had to point out this minor little benefit! Yes, when we stand before God, we will certainly be glad that we were obedient and tithed in this life. In a much smaller way and in the meantime, we will be glad every year that we tithed when we fill out our 1040s and "render unto Caesar" — or maybe surrender unto Caesar!

It's a faith builder. It's true, tithing is an illogical risk, but it strengthens your faith muscles. The more you tithe, the more God shows up, the more you trust, and the more you are willing to do things that are beautifully unsafe. Once you begin to trust your money to God, you'll see that God is faithful and true to His promises and you'll find it easier to trust Him with everything else in your life. Giving out of abundance is commendable, but giving in a time of lack emboldens and strengthens us. *"Now faith is the reality of what is hoped for, the proof of what is not seen" (Heb. 11:1).*

As we follow Christ, we'll experience days when giving goes against what we see and understand with our natural eyes. These are the times when we give in faith, knowing that God is taking care of us.

George Müller began his work by feeding, providing for, and housing orphans with two shillings in his pocket. He received the means necessary to erect great buildings and to feed orphans day by day for 60 years. Biographer J. Gilcrest Lawson recounted:

"In all that time the children did not have to go without a meal, and Mr. Müller said that if they ever had to go without a meal, he would take it as evidence that the Lord did not will the work to continue. Sometimes the meal time was almost at hand, and they did not know where the food would come from, but the Lord always sent it in due time, during the twenty thousand or more days that Mr. Müller had charge of the homes. reminds us, "Trials, obstacles, difficulties and sometimes defeats, are the very food of faith." God is our provision. When we experience the provision of God borne out of our faith; that's when amazing things happen."

It's a joy. Givers are the happiest people on the face of the earth. What image comes to mind when you think of a giver as opposed to a non-giver? The giver has an open hand and a palm facing downward. The non-giver has a tight fist; every finger gripping just as firmly as possible. Now, imagine the faces. With a non-giver, we see a scowl and frown. The giver though has a contented and open face. This is because there's a certain deep feeling of bliss that comes from giving with no regard for receiving. We realize that it wasn't ours in the first place; thus, money takes on a transcendent meaning and significance that can't be found in wealth accumulation.

> **"Givers are the happiest people on the face of the earth."**

A recent study analyzed data from a large survey and found that people who reported giving money to others or to charity were more likely to be happy, even after accounting for their income. Jesus taught this truth centuries ago when He said, *"It is more blessed to give than to receive"* (Acts 20:35).

It's unifying. Tithing can unify believers in a church. As tithers, believers are saying to God and their church family, "I'm all in." We see a beautiful, radical picture of this in the first days of the early church: *"Now the entire group of those who believed were of one heart and mind, and no one claimed that any of his possessions was his own, but instead they held everything in common"* (Acts 4:32).

Tithing husbands and wives are saying to each other, "There's something a whole lot bigger going on in our marriage than just us." Further, parents are demonstrating that same truth to their children. When children see their parents giving faithfully to the church, they get the message that God's work is a priority. Those impressions can have a life-long impact on their young minds.

It's contagious. Once tithers experience God in giving, we want to share with others about the grace and provision God has provided us. We share the joy of giving and God's graciousness to us, and others are inspired to give. If you are a pastor, minister, or leader in your church, let us encourage you to give a tithing testimony as a part of your worship service. You will want to tell how your faith has been strengthened by tithing. How has God proven Himself faithful to you? Let us offer a word of caution, though—you don't want it to sound like you are promoting a prosperity gospel, which is actually not the gospel at all. You will want to talk about the joy of giving and how God has proven Himself faithful.

It's a greed-slayer. One of the most debilitating characteristics of unhappy people is greed. And have you ever noticed it's not fun being around greedy people? There's a sense of selfishness that accompanies greed. The sad thing is that like generosity, greed can go viral. And when we feed the greed, it grows and spills over into almost every area of our lives.

One of the life-lessons we (hopefully) learn as children is the importance of sharing with others. It's not a skill that comes naturally. In fact, it seems to go against our natural inclinations. Nobody has to sit us in a classroom with a syllabus entitled: **How to Be Greedy, Session One.** Instead, somebody who cares about us, and our development as human beings teaches us that we need to share with others. That sharing builds a foundational truth that is essential for survival in life: Not everything is about us.

"Nearly all the best and most precious things in the universe you can get for a halfpenny. I make an exception, of course, of the sun, the moon, the earth, people, stars, thunderstorms, and such trifles. You can get them for nothing."
– G.K. Chesterton

It teaches an unexpected lesson. Non-tithers are often stunned by the thought that they should give up 10% of their income voluntarily to the church. They will say to themselves, "Give that kind of money to the church? We are barely getting by on what we have. We can't afford to tithe." What I have found in my own life and seen in the lives of others who have begun to tithe is that living on 90% is actually easier than living on 100%. I think it's because tithing compels me to be more mindful of what I spend and helps me be a better steward with the 90% than I would be with 100%.

> **"Have you ever noticed it's not fun being around greedy people?"**

It's biblical. Last, but not least, we give because it's a biblical principle and promise. Check out a few excerpts from the tithing narrative that God threaded throughout His Word. These are just a few of the promises and principles God gives in His Word regarding tithes and offerings. Some are from the Old Testament and others, from the New. The most familiar verse is Malachi 3:10:

THE STEWARDSHIP OF YOUR FINANCES

> *"Bring the full tenth into the storehouse so that there may be food in my house. Test me in this way," says the LORD of Armies. "See if I will not open the flood gates of heaven and pour out a blessing for you without measure."*

Notice the curious idea here. God is challenging us to test Him! It's, once again, a radical challenge to trust that God will take care of us, but even more than that, He'll will open the heaven and bless us in return. What are the blessings without measure, though? They come from Heaven, so the blessings we receive are those things far greater than money or possessions. We'll experience eternal joy, security, and purpose. Life becomes a festival of blessings rather than a dirge with our nose to an unmovable grindstone.

> *The LORD instructed Moses, "Speak to the Levites and tell them: When you receive from the Israelites the tenth that I have given you as your inheritance, you are to present part of it as an offering to the LORD – a tenth of the tenth. Your offering will be credited to you as if it were your grain from the threshing floor or the full harvest from the winepress. You are to present an offering to the LORD from every tenth you receive from the Israelites. Give some of it to the priest Aaron as an offering to the LORD. You must present the entire offering due the LORD from all your gifts. The best part of the tenth is to be consecrated. "Tell them further: Once you have presented the best part of the tenth, and it is credited to you Levites as the produce of the threshing floor or the wine press, then you and your household may eat it anywhere. It is your wage in return for your work at the tent of meeting. You will not incur guilt because of it once you have presented the best part of it, but you must not defile the Israelites' holy offerings, so that you will not die."*
> *– Num. 18:25-32*

It's interesting to note the shift from the Old Testament to the New. The writer of Hebrews calls us a chosen generation, a royal priesthood. We can look at this promise with new eyes. We see the concept of a moveable feast that we can eat anywhere! In other words, where God guides, God provides. We might seem hesitant to step out into a new ministry or geographic location. We might wonder how we're going to afford to fund the dreams we are given. We can trust that the provision is moveable as he moves us.

The point is this: The person who sows sparingly will also reap sparingly, and the person who sows generously will also reap generously. Each person should do as he has decided in his heart — not reluctantly or out of compulsion, since God loves a cheerful giver.
— 2 Cor. 9:6-7

Giving should never be a chore. It's an honor and a joy to give sacrificially. We can extend the adage and say," Where God guides, God provides, and joy resides!" There is nothing quite like seeing God move and know that you invested in the movement. At the end of our lives, we won't be asking why we gave so much but most of us will be asking ourselves why we didn't give more. So, let's be generous!

If you want to see the true character of a man, look at his bank account. Materialism is at an all-time high and generosity is at an all time low. Most economists say that todays families give less of a percentage of their income to the church and other charitable organizations than the families in the Great Depression. I really don't understand it; but I don't think I've ever met a person that has "giver's remorse" after they gave generously to the Lord. That term just doesn't exist. How could a person regret something that made them happier and changed eternity?

So as we continue to live out our lives, moment by moment, day by day, we get the opportunity to discover avenues of generosity. It's not that we *have* to give. We *get* to give!

When We Do Generosity Together

I've been a Southern Baptist church member for 54 years and I was on the cradle roll six years before that. I know all about Mission Friends, RA's and even the WMU and GA's (I went to G.A. camp in college as a lifeguard and I attended WMU meeting as a preschooler with my grandmother.) I know Children's Choir, Celebrate Life, Committees, Wednesday night Baptist business meetings and prayer meetings, green bean casseroles, Centrifuge, 5th Sunday Sings, Associations, "Victory in Jesus," Adrian Rogers, LifeWay, Lock-ins, and "Pass It On." I went to a Southern Baptist college and a Southern Baptist seminary. I have the receipts. This either sounds like I'm bragging, or I lived in a vacant classroom in my Southern Baptist church. Not true on either account. I'm just a 5th generation Southern Baptist.

But none of these things are really what makes any of us Southern Baptists. Those things are all accoutrements within Southern Baptist churches of yesteryear and some of them are still sung, attended, and experienced today. None are litmus tests. We Southern Baptists are all different and that's what makes our churches so beautiful. Our worship styles, languages, customs, service times, preaching proclivities, fall festivals, prayer rooms, summer schedules, theological nuances, and snow day policies differ.

So what's the connective tissue? With all that diversity, I've notice over the past 60 years, we do have a few rock-solid, no compromise, do or die essentials.

1. Jesus Saves
2. The Great Commission
3. Our churches are all autonomous.
4. And we work together.

The first two concepts are as broad and deep as the ocean. They are seismic in importance. Numbers three and four are lesser, but they distinguish us from other tribes. Some churches are autonomous, but they don't work together. Others work together but they aren't autonomous.

I want to camp out for a second on that last essential. When we are all in on #4, #1 and #2 are communicated loudly and clearly. One church can't send thousands of missionaries across the state, nation, and world. It's just not going to happen. But because we work together, my church is doing that. One church can't train thousands future pastors and leaders, but my church is doing that. One church can't tackle the greatest problem in the whole world: lostness. But my church is doing that. One church can't train evangelists, provide compassion, disaster relief, evangelism conferences, and a hundred other things she might care about, but my church can do that. One nondenominational church might ask, "How?" Through the Cooperative Program.

The proof is our history. The Cooperative Program fuels the greatest modern missionary movement in the world. In fact, one study recently reported that we have seven times more missionaries on the field that any other organization or denomination. And get this-- Our commissioned full-time IMB missionaries can focus on the mission rather than marketing. They don't have to fund raise, figure out pledges, sponsors, and host churches. And that's a good thing, because they weren't called to telemarketing and touring. They were created to evangelize.

The Great Commission and evangelism are the lead for Southern Baptists, but we cooperate with each other in so many other ways. When we lose our cooperative generosity, we lose what makes Southern Baptists, Southern Baptists. And when we lose our strategy of local church autonomy, we lose what makes Southern Baptists, Southern Baptists. The local church isn't dictated to by some ivory tower board room of well robed bishops telling all the churches what they have to do. In the same way, none of our churches, no matter how big they are, think that they can do all the work by themselves. Again this is just basically what it means to be a Southern Baptist. These two concepts go together like peas and carrots. That's how we "church" as Southern Baptists. And if we stray from our DNA, we're doing it wrong. We are called to reach our village, city, state, nation, and world. We can only do this by cooperating with God and cooperating with our sister churches all over the world.

Let's autonomously, diversely, cooperatively preach the word and reach the world with the gospel. And let's keep the green bean casserole recipe secret.

CHECK OUT THIS SHORT
EXPLAINER VIDEO BASED
ON THIS CHAPTER!

LORDSHIP GENEROSITY

**RESOURCEFUL WILLING
JOYFUL COURAGEOUS
GENEROUS
ETERNAL HILARIOUS
MIRACULOUS
BLESSED WORRY-FREE
JESUS IS LORD**

OR

**I AM LORD

RANDOM FEARFUL
GREEDY
INSECURE PETTY
ANXIOUS STINGY
TEMPORAL UNAVAILABLE**

LORDSHIP GENEROSITY

MOVEMENT 3
THE STEWARDSHIP OF YOUR FINANCES

- How did my money bless others this week?

- What are some expenses that I could eliminate to be a better steward?

- Am I progressing toward the goal of tithing and generosity?

- Did I bless someone financially this week? Who?

- Am I making progress toward retirement so that I can ease the burden of my family in the years to come?

- How did acts of generosity bless me this past week?

MOVEMENT 4
THE CLEANING OF THE SLATE

It all started with a mouse. Two deacons were cleaning out the storage room when a mouse scurried across the floor. Jim, a deacon in his 30's, saw the mouse and instinctively jumped and let out a scream. Larry, an older deacon, laughed and called him "a wimpy, girly man." *(Apologies to Dana Carvey's lame impression of Arnold Schwarzenegger.)* Who would have thought that an off-handed and unintended insult would lead to two years of fractured exchanges and dysfunction? It all sounds silly, right? But these things happen. A "mouse" started as a molehill but turned into a mountain. It started with verbal jabs and grew over time to evolve into a rift of resentment and broken fellowship. It seemed like Jim and Larry were always on different sides of issues in every aspect of the church. Unreconciled relationships are like a virus that can affect ministries and church fellowship, no matter how small the initial offense. How we forgive and reconcile reflects whether Jesus is really Lord or if we're just riffing on religion. Perhaps the most generous thing we will ever do is to reconcile and forgive.

Resentments Lead to Rebellion.

In most cases of broken fellowship, the root cause of the fissure begins with unsettled resentment. Even the legendary feud between the Hatfield's and McCoy's began with the selling of a single hog. Little things add up. The writer of Hebrews had a warning for the early church, *"Make sure that no one falls short of the grace of God and that no root of bitterness springs up, causing trouble and defiling many"* (Heb. 12:15). We must be proactive to make sure all resentments are crushed before they grow into something that will harm the entire church. This is sometimes tedious work, but the root must be pulled up and destroyed.

Rebellion Always Searches for Likeminded Rebels.

When resentment isn't dealt with in the individual, the next natural course is for the rebel to seek out others who share the same resentments. The rebels choose sides. The tendency of ungodly conflict is to avoid engaging with the person who has caused harm or hurt feelings or with the one with whom they disagree. No, that's too difficult. The easy way is often the most popular: to find others who share their feelings of offense. This leads to cathartic soul-bearing conversations where the rebels talk about their shared grievances. Each conversation adds another log to the ever-growing blaze. Soon, disruption or destruction results. This is how every church split begins. This pattern is also how affairs often begin. A husband holds onto a resentment against his wife and then chooses to find a woman (often in his workplace) who will listen to his pain, perhaps because he knows that her marriage is as unhealthy as his. Birds of a feather really do flock together.

> **"This is how every church split begins."**

Rebels Will Draw Swords Together.

Ultimately these rebels who harbor resentment will find a way to act on their resentments. Sometimes they climax in anger-fueled grandstanding during a business meeting that takes the pastor or moderator by surprise. In other situations, the triangulations will materialize on Facebook, Twitter, or by an anonymous letter to a leader. Once the rebels draw these kinds of swords, it's hard, but not impossible to de-escalate. It takes a peacemaker with guts who is willing to engage in a Christ-like manner in the appropriate venue. The appropriate venue is rarely the public platform. It's an honest closed-door intervention which includes prayer and listening. An interventionist doesn't have to be someone with letters behind his or her name or someone trained in conflict management. Anyone who knows how to listen, love, and discern can do this. If you are a mature believer, you have been uniquely called to this role. It's easy if you are led by the Holy Spirit. It's really hard, if not impossible, without Him. *"Do not be deceived: "Bad company corrupts good morals"* (1 Cor. 15:33).

The Fork in the Road.

When a fellowship is broken, leaders encounter a fork in the road. They can do the hard work of mending; or they can experience the heartbreaking, unbiblical practice of meandering. The church, as you know, wasn't built to meander. Mending a fellowship is a lot like setting a broken bone. It's so painful that you'd rather ignore it and just let it be. But in the end, if you don't set the bone, infection, deformity, and sometimes even the loss of a limb is the ultimate result. Jim and Larry, the major players in the mouse melee, ultimately mended their fellowship at a deacons retreat two years later. It was painful and a little public, but something amazing happened in their small church. It began to grow. That's what happens when rebels are reconciled.

PROCESS OF PERSONAL RENEWAL

Time for a quick inventory of our emotional health. The process is simple but courageous.

1. Mindfulness and Illumination

When was the last time you spent more than 15 minutes in intentional silence and stillness? Through the rush of our days, we ignore the biblical truth that God speaks in silence. He speaks softly to those who take the time to listen. He waits for us in the lonely place. We are noise hoarders; constantly filling our lives with messages and madness of the 24-hour news cycle. Sadly, we are often available to everyone who chirps on our phones or pays for the ad space, while a searching Father is longing to speak. But He will have no rivals.

Why do we trade our birthright for the stew of a chaotic and relentless collage of sounds? If we wait, He will speak. Practicing mindfulness isn't reading devotional literature, although inspirational reading is important. It's not getting through the Bible in a year, although that is admirable and reading Scripture is essential to a healthy Christian life. Mindfulness is the act of saying to God, *"Speak Lord, your servant is listening." (1 Sam. 3:10)* This is the beginning of spiritual renewal. We can't change until we stop and listen.

> **"We are noise hoarders; constantly filling our lives with messages and madness of the 24-hour news cycle."**

The Three Tenors

Let's say you wanted to hear your three favorite singers. When you arrive at the concert hall you discover that these three tenors are actually just three in a 200-voice choir of dreadfully tone-deaf singers.

You leave the concert hall demanding a refund because you really didn't get to hear what you wanted to hear. The three tenors were unheard because of the blaring dissonant sounds of less-gifted crooners.

The three tenors are the voices of the Father, the Son, and the Holy Spirit. The dissonant voices are the static and meaningless words of the day to day. At some point we must stop and find a place of silence. God's Word, silence, personal private worship, and time are elements that create an atmosphere to listen to what God has to say.

He will speak if we turn everything else off and watch and listen for Him. As believers, we must be willing to listen to His voice and invite Him to speak deeply. We need those moments when we say like David:

"Search me, God, and know my heart;
test me and know my concerns.
See if there is any offensive way in me;
lead me in the everlasting way.
— Psalm 139:23-24

If you want to do something amazing, wait. David, who was king of Israel and certainly had a zillion voices and demands vying for his attention, wrote, *"Wait for the LORD; be strong, and let your heart be courageous. Wait for the LORD"* (Ps. 27:14). David knew a valuable truth—one that applies to us still today. Your time waiting on God in silence is one of the most powerful things you can do. He speaks. But He speaks softly.

2. Repentance

"Repent" is a word we don't hear very often these days. When we do, one of two images readily come to mind. One is a red-face preacher with his finger pointed at the church ceiling and yelling, "REPENT!" The other is a street-scene of a man wearing a front-and-back sandwich board. On it are the words, "Repent, The End Is Near!"

Those images can easily be interpreted as bullying or intimidation—as condemnation or confrontation. Each conveys a sense of warning.

While a call to repent can be a warning, there's another picture we gain from Scripture, one we often overlook. The call to repent is often an invitation to life and restoration. Let's look at some of those texts:

> "This is the declaration of the Lord GOD. 'Repent and turn from all your rebellious acts, so they will not become a sinful stumbling block to you. . . For I take no pleasure in anyone's death. . . . So repent and live!'" (Ezek. 18:30,32).

> "Therefore, this is what the LORD says: If you return, I will take you back; you will stand in my presence" (Jer. 15:19).

> "The time is fulfilled, and the kingdom of God has come near. Repent and believe the good news!" (Mark 1:15).

> "Peter replied, 'Repent and be baptized, each of you, in the name of Jesus Christ for the forgiveness of your sins, and you will receive the gift of the Holy Spirit'" (Acts 2:38).

> "The Lord does not delay his promise, as some understand delay, but is patient with you, not wanting any to perish but all to come to repentance" (2 Peter 3:9).

What does it mean to repent? It is to see my sins the same way the Father does and to turn away from them as a result. Repentance thus affects both our minds and our actions, our understanding and our behavior, our head and our feet. It is not enough to feel sorry for actions that dishonor the Father; that feeling is conviction. Repentance occurs when we abandon the behavior and head in the opposite direction.

> **"Repentance occurred when they took the personally difficult step of having a conversation and each agreeing inside himself to put his hurt feelings and bitterness aside"**

I (G.B.) was teaching about this several years ago when I served as pastor for a week of children's camp north of Atlanta. To illustrate the difference in conviction and repentance I said: "It's kinda' like on Gomer Pyle, when Sgt. Carter yells, 'To the rear, march!' and all of the troops turn and head back in the opposite direction, except one. Gomer, completely clueless, continues walking in the same direction as before. He didn't change directions, thus, no repentance." I have never seen so many blank stares and confused faces. I realized that not one of those sweet, precious, little, young darlings had any idea of what or who I was talking about. Not one! I had never felt so old in my whole life!

Applying this to our story about Jim and Larry, the two may have felt for years that they needed to do something to repair their relationship. That would have been conviction. Repentance occurred when they took the personally difficult step of having a conversation and each agreeing inside himself to put his hurt feelings and bitterness aside, to lower his wall and swallow his pride, and to reach out to the other with compassion and care.

3. **Receive Forgiveness.**

John 5 tells the story of Jesus encountering a blind, lame, and paralyzed man who was beside the pool of Bethesda in Jerusalem. He had been in this condition for 38 years. Those who were sick would rest under the porticos surrounding the pool, believing the water had healing powers.

Jesus approached the man and asked, *"Do you want to get well?"* (John 5:6b) Wow! What an unusual question. This is the only time Jesus asked someone if they wanted to be healed. And it brings to mind the question: Why would Jesus ask such a question? The answer seems like it would be obvious. Jesus, though, knew the conditions of people's hearts. And some people over time seem to grow comfortable in their misery. All of us know people who are the embodiment of Gloomy Gus or Debbie Downer, don't we? As Adrian Rogers once said, "They can light up a whole room—just by leaving!"

How did the man reply? Did he say, "Absolutely! You are the miracle I have been waiting for! Surely God has sent you to me. Yes! Yes! Yes! Yes! Yes! Please do, Sir." No. Instead, he started making excuses: *"Sir, . . . I have no one to put me into the pool when the water is stirred up, but while I'm coming, someone goes down ahead of me"* (John 5:7).

Jesus, though, was not limited by what limited the man. He simply spoke, and the man was made whole. Sometimes, when we have offended someone, hurt their feelings, cheated or wronged them, we can become paralyzed by the shame of our own actions or by our pride. Trying to justify our actions, we might even tell ourselves or others, "Well, I was having a bad day" or "They deserved it!" Despite what we say though, we know we were wrong. And we become comfortable in the misery of our own wrong-doing.

Yes, we all know we are to forgive others, but let's look at the other side of this coin. How am I to respond when someone is ready to forgive me? What happens when the person we wronged reaches out with a gesture of kindness or reconciliation? Their words or actions make it obvious they are willing and ready to look beyond our offense and to forgive. How do we respond? We have a choice. Do we want to be made well? Or do we want to wallow?

Sometimes, we have difficulty receiving their forgiveness because we have not yet forgiven ourselves. Even though we have prayed and asked for God's forgiveness, sometimes we have trouble letting go of our feelings of guilt.

Guilt is the byproduct of one thing: not living up to our own expectations. That may occur because we didn't behave as we knew we ought or because we said the wrong thing. The resultant emotion is guilt.

When we have repented and asked for God's forgiveness, though, we need to accept His forgiveness as the gift that it is. Continuing to focus on our sins and guilt is essentially to put ourselves first, rather than Christ and His gift of cleansing. Sometimes, it's easier said than done. But accepting His forgiveness and cleansing is an essential element on the path of spiritual health.

So how do we put that in practice? Let's try right now. Think of an area where you have "fallen short" and asked for Christ's forgiveness. Pause for a moment, pray, and thank God for cleansing you of the stain of that sin. Thank Him for the promise based on Isaiah. 1:18: *"My sins were scarlet, stained like crimson red. Because of what Christ has done, though, they are gone and my heart and soul are as pure as fresh-fallen snow. Thank You Lord for cleansing me."* Allow yourself to sense your truly cleansed condition. Remind yourself throughout the day that you have said to Jesus, "Yes, Lord, I want to be made whole"—and rejoice in the fact that He has changed your condition.

> **"Sometimes, we have difficulty receiving their forgiveness because we have not yet forgiven ourselves."**

"Though your sins are scarlet, they will be as white as snow; though they are crimson red, they will be like wool" (Isa. 1:18).

4. Release Forgiveness

Releasing forgiveness is one of the core doctrines of our faith. Many people though, misunderstand what forgiveness really is. This is a shame, because to forgive someone is truly freeing. So, let's explore what forgiveness is, and what it is not. Let's look first at what it is not.

Forgiveness is not...

Approving bad behavior

You may have a friend or family member who has made horrible decisions that have wreaked havoc in your life. It's important for us to remember that when we forgive people, it doesn't necessarily mean that we approve of the behavior.

Enabling unacceptable actions

Enabling someone's actions can take several forms. It can be as simple as ignoring the behavior or as complex as providing money, shelter, or an alibi to the wrong doer. To enable is not an act of love; it's actually an act of cowardice. It eliminates the need to confront and allows the person to continue his or her unacceptable, hurtful, and costly actions.

A one-time event

Having to forgive someone multiple times for the same offense can be difficult. Remember, Peter asked Jesus if he was obligated to forgive a wrong-doer seven times? Jesus said, *"I tell you, not as many as seven . . . but seventy times seven"* (Matt. 18:22). The reality is that if we are keeping count, we aren't truly forgiving, are we?

We easily offer grace and forgive ourselves when we mess up—and when we mess up again in the exact same way. To be forgiving requires applying this same grace to others.

Forgetting it

"Forgive and Forget: That's my motto!" Have you ever heard someone say that? To forgive someone is not the same as forgetting what they have done, though. The more serious an offense is, the more difficult it is to forget. And some wrongs we will never forget—such as acts that were malicious, hostile, or abusive towards us or those we love. Not forgetting can actually protect us from getting ourselves into that same situation again. By remembering what has happened in the past, we can keep ourselves from experiencing that hurt again.

"Not forgetting can actually protect us from getting ourselves into that same situation again."

Trusting

We choose to forgive someone, and we offer forgiveness generously. This is good and healthy—physically, emotionally, and spiritually. Forgiving does not mean, though, that we would trust the person who wronged us to behave differently if the same circumstances were to recur. The old axiom can apply here: "There's no education in the second kick of a mule."

People earn our trust. A person who wronged us may eventually earn our trust back, but that can take time. Many factors contribute to whether we will trust that person again. In some circumstances, once that trust has been broken or violated, it might not be restored.

Now that we've defined what forgiveness is not, let's review what it is.

Forgiveness is...

A decision

Holding onto feelings of hurt, anger, or resentment can be a default response for someone who has been wronged. Forgiveness, though, involves making a conscientious decision to let go of those venomous feelings.

Rather than respond with retaliation and revenge, we can choose to offer grace and goodwill to the person who wronged us. This choice is the key to forgiving someone. The act of forgiving allows you to focus on you and your life rather than the person who hurt, disappointed, betrayed, or angered you.

So how do you forgive? You pardon the person. If, as mentioned above, guilt comes because we did not live up to our own expectations, then an offense comes because someone else did not live up to our expectations. To forgive means to let go of the hurt feelings we have felt because of another person's past actions. We accept the fact that we cannot change the past, undo someone else's wrongdoing, or unhear their hurtful words. Forgiving keeps us from becoming bogged down in negativity because of what someone else did.

> **"Choosing to forgive breaks the chain that binds us to the past hurtful event."**

A gift we give ourselves

We easily think that we forgive a person for the benefit of the one who has wronged or offended us. This, though, is not the case. Our forgiving someone is for our own benefit. Not forgiving the person keeps us tied to the past; it anchors us to a by-gone event. Continuing to focus on the offense means we choose to live looking backwards.

Interestingly, the person who has offended us has moved on

with his or her life. They likely have found a way to incorporate their action into their life-history—or maybe they didn't give it a second thought to begin with. This means that while their actions may keep you up at night, the offender sleeps soundly.

Someone has said that holding onto bitterness and hatred is like drinking poison and hoping the other person gets sick. The same happens when we fail to forgive; it hurts us.

Choosing to forgive breaks the chain that binds us to the past hurtful event. Forgiving someone frees up the energy it takes to bear the burden of anger indefinitely. It allows us to put the baggage down and move forward.

How does forgiving someone benefit us? It can help us feel better about ourselves—not in an "I'm a superior person" kind of way but in a "This actually does improve my life" kind of way. Physically, to forgive helps to lower our blood pressure and helps us feel less anxious. This is good for both the heart and the mind. Letting go of the hurtful baggage releases the shadow of depression that easily accompanies hurt feelings and disappointment.

A gift we give to those we love

Our holding onto a past hurt keeps us from living in the joy and enjoyment of the present moment. Not forgiving someone casts a shadow over our current lives and affects our current relationships—even with those who were not at all involved in the hurtful situation. Our other relationships suffer collateral damage when we fail to forgive someone.

A clue that we have not forgiven someone can come when we find ourselves overreacting in a totally unrelated situation. When something minor happens, a negative event that might call for a sane and quiet response and instead we drop an emotional neutron bomb, this is a clue that something else is bothering us. We have displaced our train-car load of anger or disappointment onto a thimble-sized event. Those kinds of reactions negatively affect our relationships with others. Nobody wants to sit next to a hand-grenade and wonder when it's going to go off.

A reflection of God's character

A vivid memory that stands clear in my mind (G.B.'s) is of seeing a bulletin board in the children's department in Sunday School. It had a picture of a child's face in the upper right-hand corner and part of a verse filling up the rest of the space. It simply said, "Be ye kind one to another."

Many times, I have recalled that image, those words, and the rest of that verse. In full context, it says, *"And be kind and compassionate to one another, forgiving one another, just as God also forgave you in Christ"* (Eph. 4:32).

When I graduated seminary, my wife and I were appointed as Church Planter Apprentices with the then Home Mission Board (now the North American Mission Board or NAMB). One of our training leaders talked about handling conflict and quoted this verse. I'll not soon forget the trainer's words: "It doesn't cost anything to be kind, tenderhearted, and forgiving. Not being so can cost you everything." I have to admit that I have not always scored 100% on that; but I have tried to make it my practice.

"Nobody wants to sit next to a hand-grenade and wonder when it's going to go off."

The Bible says much about God's forgiving nature. Because He has forgiven all our sins, we should not withhold forgiveness from others. Here's a snapshot of some of the promises relating to Christ's perfect willingness to forgive our sins and offenses:

- *He forgives them all.* (I John 1:9)
- *He casts them into the sea.* (Micah 7:9)
- *He takes them away.* (Isaiah 6:7)
- *He covers them up.* (Psalm 32:1)
- *He blots them out.* (Acts 3:19)
- *He puts them away.* (Hebrews 9:26)
- *He remembers them no more.* (Hebrews 8:12)

You will never be more like Christ than when you forgive someone who has hurt or betrayed you. The striking example of Jesus's willingness to forgive occurred when He interceded for those who crucified Him: *"Father, forgive them, because they do not know what they are doing"* (Luke 23:34). If He can forgive them, then certainly . . . .

Extreme Forgiveness

Two biblical examples illustrate radical forgiveness. The first is the story of Joseph forgiving his brothers who had sold him into slavery years earlier. When he finally revealed himself to his brothers, *"Joseph kissed each of his brothers and wept"* (Gen. 45:15). That was a moment of extreme forgiveness!

The second story is the well-known parable of the prodigal son (Luke 15:11-32). Culturally, two details stand out in this story. First, in asking for his inheritance, the younger son was, in essence, saying to his father, "I wish you were dead." Jesus's first-century hearers would have understood this implication and would have been outraged by such a hate-filled and self-centered request. Despite what the son said and did afterwards, the father was ready and wanting to welcome him home. We know that because, *"while the son was still a long way off, his father saw him and was filled with compassion. He ran, threw his arms around his neck, and kissed him"* (Luke 15:20). Again, Jesus's hearers would have been shocked by this sentence. Why? Jewish men of the first century NEVER ran.

Children ran. Slaves ran. Women might run. But men? Never. It was considered undignified and degrading. Why did the father run? Yes, he was excited to see his son. He also may have been wanting to protect his son from being accosted by neighbors in the village who would have known what he had done. The father was willing to go against the cultural norms and willing to risk public humiliation so he could be reunited with his wayward son. He was willing to forgive—regardless. It was extreme forgiveness put into action.

The world might not understand why we are willing to forgive someone who has wronged us. We are not called to live by culture's standards, though, are we? Because the Lord has forgiven our sins, we should never withhold our forgiveness from others—regardless.

5. Worship Him

Forgiveness is a big deal in Jesus' eyes, and it's connected to what Jesus taught and lived. To see someone who refuses to forgive is to see someone living outside the will and worship of God. It's all about forgiveness. And once you receive forgiveness and release forgiveness, you can't help but worship. We are overwhelmed with God's goodness because a load is lifted. Imagine you're reading the Bible, the part where Jesus talks in the New Testament. He's always going on about forgiveness and why it matters. Like that time that He gave folks the Lord's Prayer lesson (Matt. 6:9-15). He told them to ask for forgiveness just as they forgive others. So, it's like a two-way street: you want forgiveness, you must give it too.

> **"You will never be more like Christ than when you forgive someone who has hurt or betrayed you."**

But here's the kicker: Jesus was all about showing love and forgiveness, even to the folks who treated Him badly. So, when we say you should forgive before worshiping Jesus, it's because we're following His example. We can recall how Jesus continually forgave those that crucified Him and remember that this is our model. That's what we're going for.

Forgiving others clears the air between you and God. If you're holding onto grudges and anger, it's like putting a wall between you and God. By forgiving, you're hitting the reset button and making your connection with God stronger. Plus, if you hold onto grudges, it can make you bitter and negative. That's not a good look. Forgiveness is a way to let go of all that negativity and start fresh.

> **"Worship is the delight and the dessert of forgiveness."**

In other words, you worship. You praise God that you were forgiven, and you worship Him for giving you the power to forgive. Worship is the delight and the dessert of forgiveness.

And here's the cool part: forgiving can mend broken friendships. The whole message of the gospel is reconciling broken things and recreating, resurrecting, and reclaiming relationships that are in shambles.

Just so you know, you must forgive before you worship, while others might believe that Jesus forgives you no matter what. But no matter how you slice it, forgiveness is the metanarrative of gospel. After we release forgiveness, we are ready to worship Jesus.

Caution

So, what is the danger of living with an unclean slate? Samson discovered that in Judges 16:20: *"Then she cried, 'Samson, the Philistines are here!' When he awoke from his sleep, he said, 'I will escape as I did before and shake myself free.' But he did not know that the Lord had left him."*

What a rude awakening! Literally!

What are a few modern examples of this sudden exit?

- He tweeted (or should I say "X-ed") a hot take (opinion) and he didn't know the Lord had left him.
- He took pleasure in the failures of someone, and he didn't know the Lord had left him.
- He longed for the admiration of others, and he didn't know the Lord had left him.
- He spent so long criticizing a colleague that he didn't know the Lord had left him.
- He resented his wife because of a comment or a failure and he didn't know the Lord had left him.

A Parable

Last week I was praying about a very important conversation I needed to have with one of my many supervisors. (I seem to collect quite a few.) For several weeks I had been struggling with an issue. I also worried about the conversation.

- *How would he react?*
- *Will he pushback on my observations and concerns?*
- *Will I speak the truth?*
- *Will he think poorly of me?*
- *Is it really worth his time?*

I can do this for extended periods of time. My OCD in third gear, I suppose. I have a reputation of being non-confrontational, so this was a very important and nerve-racking phone call. I finally got the courage to make the call on a long road trip. Although I was skeptical about whether this was the right time or if it would it be better for me to have a face-to-face meeting with him. We began the conversation, and everything was cordial and upbeat and then I broached the uncomfortable subject. My monologue went on for about five minutes and then I asked a question. Silence filled the space where I expected to get feedback or even a rebuttal.

THE CLEANING OF THE SLATE

I nervously rambled a little more and then a little more. I asked another question. Still silence. It was at that moment I realized that the call had dropped in the middle of my conversation. In fact, my manager tried to call me back, but I didn't look at who the caller was. I just kept rambling and ignorantly assumed that my manager was listening intently.

This slightly embarrassing slice of my life reminded me of a much larger meta-story. I thought about the fact that many times as I go through my day I can get so wrapped up in my own diatribes, anecdotes, and amusements that I fail to realize that the Holy Spirit left the building. This was Samson's predicament. He was a man of great strength but in that moment, he forgot where his strength came from and experienced the sudden realization that he had no strength because the Lord had left him. The worst thing that could happen to any of us would be for God to leave us to our own futile strategies and schemes. A dropped call might be embarrassing for a moment but realizing that the Lord slipped out of the room at your time of greatest need reeks of tragedy and despair. The Lord's presence strengthens us to do things that we could never do, while the Lord's absence only leads to our demise.

This happens with churches, too. We get so caught up in our own problems, glory, issues, budgets, concerns, activities, and structures that when we finally stop for a short second, we come to realize that the Holy Spirit has left the building. When things get flesh-saturated, He might just slip out the door and find another place where the focus is on God and not on our man-made idols and edicts.

Step away.
Be still.
Listen.
Stop talking.
Make space.

Question everything.
Let go.
Let God.

CHECK OUT THIS SHORT
EXPLAINER VIDEO BASED
ON THIS CHAPTER!

TRUTH-BASED ACCEPTED HONEST LOVING MERCIFUL COMMUNICATED AVAILABLE GRACE-FUELED CELEBRATED EMPATHETIC

JESUS IS LORD

OR

I AM LORD

CIRCUMSTANTIAL CYCLICAL TRIANGULATION VENGEFUL SHAME-BASED DESPONDENCY BITTER UNFORGIVING FROZEN VOLATILE DISCONNECTED

LORDSHIP GENEROSITY

MOVEMENT 4
CLEANING OF THE SLATE

- Is there a relationship in my life that took a hit this week?

- What wounding needs healing during this season of my life in relationships and conflict?

- In what ways have I broken the heart of God through my relationships?

- What steps did I take this week to seek reconciliation?

- How did God speak to me regarding my emotions? What do I sense Him saying to me about my emotional health?

MOVEMENT 5
THE STORY OF YOUR LIFE

Here's the Good News. You get to write the theme of your story. With each decision you make, with each person you encounter, with every dollar you give, and every minute you serve, you are writing the story of your life. Every facet matters! We get a chance to steward our story in every day and activity. It's how our lives become generous and it's how we make Jesus the main character and theme of our lives. It's how we make him LORD.

When we are living out our story, we must decide what role we will play in the much larger story - God's story. God's story has a running theme of generosity and lordship. Through our actions we are communicating our own view of Who is really Lord.

There's something going on in the heart of every person. It's universal. It escorts us nightly through vivid three-dimensional dreams. It draws into dark rooms to observe the flickering lights of a movie. We turn pages filled with words that transport us to undiscovered experiences. This is the power of story. God created us for story. That's why He gave us a Book. It's filled with a cast of characters that inform us of the nature of life in all its aspects. Heroes, villains, guides, and dramatic arcs… They're all there. Consider the incredible story of the orphan queen Esther.

The Role of the Villain: Haman

When Haman saw that Mordecai was not bowing down or paying him homage, he was filled with rage.
— Esther 3:5

Haman is the classic villain. He lusts for power and payback. Cursed with a sort of familiar narcissism, he longs to be the leading character. He plots with stealth, abhorring correction or criticism. Just like Haman, the narcissist in your life wants the glory. He saturates his conversations with talk of his importance. He relies heavily on alternative facts that are shallow, baseless, and usually pointless. He's ruthlessly at work creating allies and desires to control both the people and the narrative. If you want to see the exact opposite of Lordship Generosity, look no further than Haman! We can all relate to a villain like this and most people have a few of them in their personal world. Villains in your story will always challenge lordship generosity.

> **"When villains are pulling strings we all need a faithful Mordecai."**

The Role of the Guide: Mordecai

Esther's response was reported to Mordecai. Mordecai told the messenger to reply to Esther, "Don't think that you will escape the fate of all the Jews because you are in the king's palace. If you keep silent at this time, relief and deliverance will come to the Jewish people from another place, but you and your father's family will be destroyed. Who knows, perhaps you have come to your royal position for such a time as this."
— Esther 4:12-14

Like the wise Obi-Wan Kenobi, Mordecai sees the big picture and challenges Esther to rise beyond her own insecurities, fears, and apprehensions. He calls her to adventure. We all need someone to call us out of our normal world into a divine saga. Everyone needs that voice in their lives to challenge us to be more than we thought we could be. When villains are pulling strings we all need a faithful Mordecai. Everyone needs wise counsel.

His words to Esther were engraved in immortality. *"For such a time as this…"* Grand moments are rare and often come unexpectedly. And when they come, the hero seizes them. A hero must nurture an expectant heart willing to strike at the right time. Sometimes destinies are lost because we'd rather watch television.

The Role of the Prayer Warrior

Esther sent this reply to Mordecai: "Go and assemble all the Jews who can be found in Susa and fast for me. Don't eat or drink for three days, night or day. I and my female servants will also fast in the same way. After that, I will go to the king even if it is against the law. If I perish, I perish." So Mordecai went and did everything Esther had commanded him.
— Esther 4:15-17

Prayer comes before action. Divine intervention triggers divine action. The gods of Rome and Greece were fickle aberrations. King, queens, and pawns were subject to the whims of the lusts and moods of their gods. Our faith is in the God who calls us into the adventure. But not as a lone warrior. He bids us into partnership. Prayer becomes our connecting point.

One other interesting fact: The rabbis of the Talmud suggest that during this time of fasting and prayer, Esther's recurring context and motif as she prayed was this: *My God, My God, why have You forsaken me.* Also, the length of the fast, three days further, links the plight of salvation from Haman to the plight of our own salvation accomplished through Jesus.

The Mystery of Divine Intervention

That night sleep escaped the king, so he ordered the book recording daily events to be brought and read to the king (Esth. 6:1).

There is an unseen hand that sculpts the story. He wakes people up in the middle of the night to do his work. The people prayed and a king had insomnia. So, what does a king do when he's awake in the middle of the night? He wants to read about himself. Because of this biographical work, the king discovers that the outsider, the rebel who refused to follow the party line, Mordecai, is actually a hero.

The Unexpected Twist

Haman entered, and the king asked him, "What should be done for the man the king wants to honor?" (Esth. 6:6).

Every great story has a hairpin turn where black is suddenly white and white is suddenly black. The dialogue is filled with humor and ironic consequence. Haman assumes all the wrong things, as villains usually do in great stories. All the accolades Haman suggests to the king end up in the lap of Mordecai. And all the plans Haman had for Mordecai end up on the head of himself.

The Triumphant End

Mordecai went from the king's presence clothed in royal blue and white, with a great gold crown and a purple robe of fine linen. The city of Susa shouted and rejoiced (Esth. 8:15).

The day of gallows and glory is coming. Those who have suffered unjustly will be vindicated. And those who prefer the role of villain will receive the fruit of their foiled mission. We all have a choice as to which role we will play.

It's not fair to the larger story for you to wait in the wings by putting down the sword, remaining stuck, fearful, and distracted, when there is a world of adventure right outside the door of your iron and moated castle. The adventure is yours.

For the Glory of God

Throughout the Gospels, Jesus warned people to watch out for phonies. *"Be on your guard against false prophets who come to you in sheep's clothing but inwardly are ravaging wolves"* (Matt. 7:15). Jesus wasn't talking about the Romans, the tax collectors, or the prostitutes. He spoke these words about the leaders in the temple. These men prayed in public places like thespians, full of style but with a major substance crisis.

> **"And those who prefer the role of villain will receive the fruit of their foiled mission."**

Their prayers weren't meant for the ears of God. They were for the ears of men. They were mask enthusiasts. They loved holiness masks, self-righteous masks, blame masks, God masks, leader masks, supernatural masks, liturgical masks, public worship masks, power masks, elite masks, perfection masks, Sabbath style masks, sacrifice masks, rule masks, and a few dozen others.

These were the glory thieves. What made them so dangerous was they looked the part according to the world's standards but, as Jesus said, they were whitewashed tombs. They looked good on the outside but on the inside, they were merely religious skullduggery. They found glory in themselves. They memorized all the laws and loopholes. They thought that was enough. But as we look deeper and discover who God is through the life of Jesus, we realize that it's always been about love, not laws. It's love that fosters godly living and drives us back to the throne of God to give Him glory.

When we experience the wonder of God, we can do nothing other than to thrive in His glory and not our own. Every Christ-follower becomes a sojourner to the throne, and the closer we get to the glory of God, the more we are marked by the luminous power of His grace and glory. We move from glory thief to glory giver. So, what does it look like when we give God glory? Here are four characteristics of the glory giver.

The one who gives God glory is marked by complete surrender.

Paul said it best: *"Therefore, brothers and sisters, in view of the mercies of God, I urge you to present your bodies as a living sacrifice, holy and pleasing to God; this is your true worship"* (Rom. 12:1).

When we see an athlete totally committed to victory, we often say, "He (or she) left all on the field." The imagery here is a picture of someone who didn't hold back an ounce of energy or focus. I believe this is what Paul meant. A fully devoted follower of Christ is selflessly offering his or her life on the altar for God's glory. The Christ-follower says, "I am surrendering absolutely everything for You, Jesus and I do this, not for the praise of men or the approval of my peers. I am surrendering everything so that people will glorify You."

> **"They were whitewashed tombs. They looked good on the outside but on the inside, they were merely religious skullduggery."**

The person who gives God glory is marked by a passion for people.

What are the three things God cares most about? It's simple. People, people, and people. We bring glory to God when our top priority is to see people join us in following Him. Jesus was wrecked by the lostness around Him. We hear the pathos as He mourns over them, crying out, *"Jerusalem, Jerusalem, who kills the prophets and stones those who are sent to her. How often I wanted to gather your children together, as a hen gathers her chicks under her wings, but you were not willing!" (Matt. 23:37)*. When we grieve over the lostness of people, we connect to the heart of Christ, and unfurl the banner of His glory.

That passion for people also moves us to show them compassion in Christ's name. We feed the hungry, give drink to the thirsty, clothe the naked, give lodging to the stranger, and visit the prisoner and the sick. The result is that people's lives are touched, their destinies are changed, and Christ's name is glorified.

The person who gives God glory is marked by radical generosity.

We live in a culture that bows down at the altar of money and possessions. When we are radically committed to generosity, we reflect the One who so loves the world that He gave. Too often the world thinks the message of Christianity is "give so that you get." While it's true that God takes care of us when we give, the real message is that we give to glorify God. Jesus knew that one of the greatest heart barometers is our financial stewardship. Are we willing to follow Him rather than money? Jesus said, *"No one can serve two masters, since either he will hate one and love the other, or he will be devoted to one and despise the other. You cannot serve both God and money" (Matt. 6:24)*.

The person who gives glory to God is marked by extraordinary faith.

If we listen closely to the whisper of God in every uncertainty and fiery trial, we can hear Him ask, "Do you trust Me?" The unexpected diagnosis: "Do you trust Me?" The prodigal daughter: "Do you trust Me?" The loss of a job: "Do you trust Me?" The valley of depression: "Do you trust Me?" The writer of Hebrews reminds us that *"Without faith it is impossible to please God, since the one who draws near to him must believe that He exists and that he rewards those who seek him" (Heb. 11:6)*. When we have extraordinary faith in hard places, we glorify God. So often, it is not our successes but our extraordinary faith in adversity that brings Him glory. The pages of Scripture pour out story after story of imperfect people who brought glory to Him through enduring faith. Our darkest hour in the eyes of the world can be our finest hour is the eyes of God.

So when you reach the end of your life, what story do you want to tell? This question should be considered with every decision and plan. Will this story, in the end, bring God glory?

CHECK OUT THIS SHORT
EXPLAINER VIDEO BASED
ON THIS CHAPTER!

**HEROIC UNENDING
ADVENTURE MEANINGFUL
TRANSCENDENT
THEMATIC SHAREABLE
FAITH-FOCUSED**

JESUS IS LORD

or

I AM LORD

**RANDOM VICTIM
DOUBTFUL SECRETIVE
SELF-AGGRANDIZING
LIMITED INCOMPLETE
FALSE PRIDEFUL VAIN**

LORDSHIP GENEROSITY

MOVEMENT 5
THE STORY OF YOUR LIFE

- What role did I play in God's bigger story this week?

- What did I do this week to make my story a God-glorifying one?

- With whom did I share a part of my story this past week?

- With whom did I share God's big story this week?

- How did the enemy try to sabotage my story last week?

MOVEMENT 6
THE IMPACT OF YOUR LEGACY
BY TOD TANNER

Farming is not easy work; this is probably why many people do not farm. The farmer works long hours in the expectation that the work will not be in vain. He will put seed in the ground in the hopes that it will yield a large crop in the future. The yield will also be dependent upon the amount of labor the farmer puts in between the planting and the harvest. Then, when the harvest is had, the farmer must return to the field to prepare the field for next year's crop. If the farmer desires to have a great harvest, he must be intentional in his actions throughout the process.

Building an estate plan can be like farming, in that it calls for intentional work. Furthermore, the person putting the estate plan together is putting in the work with the hopes of something beyond the now. The farmer plants seed knowing that a harvest will come. The person putting an estate plan together does so knowing that the work today will benefit others in the future.

The goal in this chapter is to better understand the estate planning process. When we understand something better, then we are more apt to apply our newfound knowledge. In seeking to grow our understanding, we will learn how estate planning is truly a part of Lordship generosity. In this chapter we will learn who needs an estate plan, the documents that make up an estate plan, the tax advantages that can be had with an estate plan, along with the impact an estate plan can have beyond our lifetimes. Let's begin our journey.

Estate Planning and Lordship Generosity

The apostle Paul was one of the greatest missionaries of all time. He traveled the known world of his time telling others about Jesus. In his missionary journeys, he would plant churches and seek to strengthen existing churches. One church that he took a great deal of interest in was the church at Corinth. In his second letter to them he stated, *"The person who sows sparingly will also reap sparingly, and the person who sows generously will also reap generously. Each person should do as he has decided in his heart – not reluctantly or out of compulsion, since God loves a cheerful giver"* (2 Cor. 9:6-7).

Paul used an agrarian metaphor when talking about generosity and giving. If we sow sparingly, then we will reap sparingly. If we sow abundantly, then we will reap abundantly. It is vital to understand that a great deal takes place between the time of sowing and reaping. We once again see that farming is hard work.

What if we take this concept and apply it to estate planning? What does it look like for us to see our estates through the lens of sowing and reaping? It is possible to build our estate plans in such a way that we can literally give to Kingdom-minded ministries until the return of Christ? This is not contingent on the amount of funds we currently have or the amount of funds we may leave behind. Instead, it is contingent on our heart's desire to see the Kingdom of God advanced beyond our lifetimes.

Paul taught the church at Corinth this exact principle when he said each person needed to decide in his own heart how he was going to sow. The first truth we learn from this passage is that estate planning with Lordship generosity is a personal choice. Paul did not tell the church at Corinth that this was a decision to be made by the church body or a committee from within the church. Instead, it was a personal decision. When a decision like this is made as a group, it is easy for individuals within the group to recant. When a decision like this is made individually, the individual knows that accountability to the decision is lived out personally.

Secondly, we learn that this is a decision to be made within someone's heart. In studying the New Testament, the heart represents the center of someone's being and communicates the true intent of that person's convictions. When a decision is made at the heart level, the actions are much more apt to be lived out because the decision itself is a conviction.

Finally, we learn that the decision is not to be made reluctantly or under compulsion. Many of us have heard the term groupthink. Groupthink occurs when a host of people make the same decision without reflecting upon the decision itself. If someone is pressed to give an account of why they decided something during a time of groupthink, the response will be because everyone else was doing the same thing. Putting together an estate plan with Lordship Generosity in heart and mind is not to be done under compulsion, but rather cheerfully as the impact will have eternal implications.

Who Needs an Estate Plan?

'When thinking about putting an estate plan together, two common misconceptions tend to present themselves. First, people will say that they do not have enough resources to need an estate plan. This misconception is built upon the false premise that an estate plan is only for wealthy people. Furthermore, one wrongly concludes that what someone has within their wallet or bank accounts is the total of their estate.

To offset this false belief, we must fully comprehend what makes up one's estate. An individual's bank account(s) typically represents 3% of an estate. The remaining 97% is found in retirement plans, life insurance policies, the equity in one's home, cars, and all the remaining material possessions. When someone begins to look at their estate through this lens, then that individual begins to have an accurate picture of how grand their estate truly is.

The second common misconception is that estate planning is only for those who are in their golden years. This would be accurate if we all knew when we were going to called home to glory or when Jesus was going to return. The truth, however, is that we do not know when this will take place. Therefore, we need to think about estate planning, no matter our age.

To further accentuate this point, let's discuss a possible scenario. Let's say that a young couple with children dropped the kids off with the grandparents and went out on a much-needed date night. The night, however, turned tragic and the couple was called home to glory. If the couple had an estate plan in place, then the children would immediately have guardians to whom they could go, and the healing process could begin. If, however, they did not have an estate plan, then the court would begin to make needed decisions. Sure, they would probably go to the grandparents. But this unnecessary step, involving additional litigation, could have been avoided.

> **"We need to think about estate planning, no matter our age."**

As followers of Jesus, we understand that we are in this world for only a short period of time. At some point, Jesus is either calling His church home or we will slip into eternity. Since we know this to be true, it would only make sense for us to plan for either event. Yet, research over the years has yielded the same statistic. Almost 70% of those who pass away do so without an estate plan.

If you happen to be one of many people who do not have an estate plan, it may be helpful for you to know what would happen to your loved ones if you were to pass away. The short answer is that the state would step in and start making the decisions on your behalf. You can be confident that your spouse or heirs will represent your intentions to the court when the time arrives. You can also be confident that the court does not have to respond to any of their wishes or statements.

Another setback for those without an estate plan is increased costs. Loved ones will need to hire legal counsel to open, manage, and close the estate. Loved ones will be required to spend additional hours with said counsel in court before a judge. This may not be argumentative time, but it could be. No matter if everyone is polite or not, it will be expensive time. This cost, however, can all be handled in the now if someone puts together an estate plan.

> "The reality is that we own nothing, and God is the owner of everything. If we truly believe this, then we will want to steward or manage His resources well."

One last point regarding this matter is that most of us would rather make decisions regarding the stewardship of the possessions the Lord has entrusted to us be made by us and not the state. The reality is that we own nothing, and God is the owner of everything. If we truly believe this, then we will want to steward or manage His resources well. When we delay in making an estate plan, then we are more apt to allow the state to do what God has called us to do.

What's In an Estate Plan?

Now that we know that everyone needs an estate plan, it is time to start building one. An estate plan is going to require at least four documents and each document accomplishes a specific and needed task. Three of the four documents are needed when someone is alive, and the fourth document takes precedence when a person passes away. The documents needed while alive are a living will, a medical power of attorney, and a financial power of attorney. The document that is needed upon the passing of an individual is a last will and testament. Let's learn about each of these documents and what they accomplish.

A living will, which can also be called an advance directive for health care, allows each person to predetermine what care they wish to receive when the end of life is at hand. Does a person want to be kept alive via life support systems? Does an individual desire to be kept alive via a feeding tube or receive additional lifesaving care at the ending stages of an illness? While these are difficult questions to ponder, it is best to ponder these questions in the now rather than when the situation is taking place.

We can find at least two reasons for wanting to complete a living will. First, this document can be a gift to our loved ones. When we make these decisions, then our loved ones do not have to make them on our behalf. A second benefit is that when our wishes are communicated in writing and then our wishes will be honored. If a living will is needed but has not been executed, then the laws of your state where you live will determine who may make decisions on your behalf. It does not matter if our loved ones state that we would not want to be kept alive via life support. The doctors will not act until they have legal standing. Therefore, our loved ones will have added stress in an already difficult situation.

We can look at the next two documents together as they are similar in nature. The medical power of attorney gives an individual the authority to make medical decisions when you are unable to make medical decisions. For example, if someone has surgery and medical decisions need to be made, the person who has been given the authority can do so until the individual has recovered and is able to make his or her own decisions. Likewise, a financial power of attorney grants similar rights. It is not uncommon to see a financial power of attorney used when someone is experiencing dementia or Alzheimer's. Under these circumstances, a patient may have been placed in assisted living or memory care. The individual given the authority via the financial power of attorney can make all decisions necessary to make sure the patient has the needed resources available to provide for his or her needed care.

The final document needed to make up an estate plan is someone's last will and testament. The overall objective of this document is to clearly articulate one's wishes and desires upon one's passing. As we have already learned, someone's overall estate is much more than what someone has within various bank accounts. The last will and testament will take into consideration someone's total estate and provides legal standing for decisions moving forward.

Most of us would acknowledge that our most valuable treasure is not our possessions, but rather our loved ones and especially our children. If someone is of the age in which they still have children at home, the last will and testament takes on an even greater priority. Parents have a responsibility to make sure that their young children are taken care of financially, emotionally, and physically. The last will and testament is the place in which a trust is built, trustees are named, and guardianship is determined. Once again, if this is not done, then the state will begin to make these decisions. Even if the state has the best interest for the children at heart, they are not equipped to make this decision as they do not know the children nor the extended family. The parents are best equipped for this, and parents have a calling to provide for their children in this manner.

One final benefit for a last will and testament is that it affords a follower of Jesus one last chance to share his or her testimony. Many Christians have been known to start their will acknowledging Jesus as Lord and Savior and affirming his or her faith in Christ, yet again. As loved ones are studying and implementing the desires expressed in the will, they will see a clear and concise account of the fact that we cannot take any of our worldly possessions with us into eternity. The only thing that truly matters in the end is where we stand with Jesus Christ.

Benefits of an Estate Plan

We have learned that everyone needs an estate plan and we

have learned of the documents that make up an estate plan. The last step we need to take is understanding the benefits associated with having an estate plan. We have already discovered the benefits of the three documents that are needed while we are living, that being the advance care directive and the two power of attorney documents. This section will discuss three primary benefits related to the last will and testament.

> "The oldest child may be the best choice or the oldest child may also be the worst choice."

The first benefit is that the individual putting together a last will and testament can name the person who will be responsible for carrying out all the plans outlined in the document. This person is called the executor of the will. If someone is married, the spouse typically fulfills this responsibility. If, however, someone is not married or is the last to pass away from that family, then someone else is called upon to fill this roll.

Choosing someone to serve as the executor is an important decision. Sometimes married couples may say that the oldest living child is supposed to be the executor. The oldest child may be the best choice or the oldest child may also be the worst choice. Executorship is best fulfilled by someone who has the needed time, is strong with details, and is willing to honor the wishes of the person who passed, as outlined in the will.

Sometimes the best person to fulfill the responsibilities of executorship is someone outside the immediate family. It has been said that money can magnify circumstances. If the circumstances within a family are loving, then the passing of a person and distribution of his or her assets can be a celebration. If, however, the family circumstances are unfavorable, then the distribution of someone's assets can be difficult and it is best to have a third party serve as executor. Each family is unique, and it is best for the executor to be prayerfully considered.

The second benefit is related to taxes. Depending on the size of the overall estate, steps can be taken via the will to limit or even eliminate tax liability. For example, if a husband or wife wants to ensure that the remaining spouse is taken care of at their passing, the will can build what is known as a charitable remainder trust. A charitable remainder trust accomplishes several objectives. First, it will generate a consistent and steady line of income for the remaining spouse. Upon the passing of the first spouse, money from his or her estate goes into a trust. This trust, in turn will generate regularly scheduled distribution checks for the remaining spouse and can do this until the passing of the remaining spouse. The trust can also be crafted to give to another generation of beneficiaries up to 20 years beyond the last spouse's passing.

The second benefit to creating a charitable remainder trust is that the assets that are used to fund this trust are not taxed upon the building of the trust. If someone has a sizable estate, an estate tax may be applied to the estate. Some or all these estate taxes can be avoided through the funding of a charitable remainder trust. It is important to consult an estate attorney or a CPA to determine when an estate tax is likely as the numbers vary from year-to-year.

The final benefit to creating a charitable remainder trust is found in the name. When the trust is built, funds are given to the trust and these funds are invested. As the funds grow, distributions are based on actuary tables. Upon the passing of the remaining spouse or the 20 years, if the distributions are going to the second generation, whatever is remaining within the trust goes to the charity chosen by the person who contributed to the original amount. The charity can be the person's home church, a missions organization, or any other 501(c)(3). This is one way for someone to give to ministries of his or her choice beyond their lifetime.

Finally, creating a last will and testament allows a person to give to Kingdom causes one last time. We have learned throughout this journey that God is the owner of everything, and we are merely the stewards. We have also learned the importance of tithing and how God calls us to test Him on this and see if He does not pour out His blessings upon those who faithfully tithe. Knowing all of this to be factual, what would it look like to tithe our estate? If someone was to do this, the last will and testament would be the place to articulate this wish.

Tithing your estate can take on one of two options. First, someone could simply state that they desire to leave a certain percentage of their estate to their home church or other Christ-centered cause. When the will is written this way, the desired portion of the estate goes to the church or ministry as a one-time gift.

A second option would be to use funds from an estate and form a permanent endowment. When someone choses this option, a portion of an estate is used to build a permanent endowment. This endowment is managed by a ministry like the Tennessee Baptist Foundation.

The Foundation is responsible for investing the funds and providing distributions of the funds to the ministries as outlined in the will itself. Unlike the one-time check, funds from this endowment will be distributed on a regular basis, literally until the return of Christ. If Jesus waits a thousand years to come and get His bride, funds from this endowment will still be giving to the ministries as outlined in the will.

It's easier than you think!

Doing an estate plan can be scary. The subject matter can cause fear because we do not like to think about the end of our lives here on earth. Reality is that we are all going to pass away at some point. Therefore, we need to take necessary steps to prepare for the inevitable and take care of our loved ones at the time of our passing. Failing to do so will lead to unnecessary struggle during a difficult time.

Another reason that putting together an estate plan can be scary, is because we do not understand the language or everything that goes into an estate plan. Let this chapter serve as a tutor for what goes into an estate plan. Your next step is to find a trusted advisor who can walk with you step by step so that you can build a plan that meets your needs and honors the One who has saved you.

We now have a choice. We can either continue to let fear stop us from building an estate plan or we can start taking the steps needed to build one. We do not have to build a complete plan in a day, as this is an unrealistic expectation. But we can start the journey today. Before the day is over, write down a name or two of someone you can call to ask for help. Then, when tomorrow comes, make a call and start the journey.

> **"Creating a last will and testament allows a person to give to Kingdom causes one last time."**

CHECK OUT THIS SHORT EXPLAINER VIDEO BASED ON THIS CHAPTER!

LORDSHIP GENEROSITY

THE IMPACT OF YOUR LEGACY

**FAR-REACHING TRIUMPHANT
GOD-HONORING
DIVINE SEISMIC
PROVISION ENDOWING
LIFE-ALTERING CONTINUING
HEAVEN-FOCUSED**

JESUS IS LORD

— OR —

I AM LORD

**POWERLESS WASTED
SMALL INSIGNIFICANT
PURPOSELESS DECAYING
DESOLATION HAVOC MAKING
MEANINGLESS**

LORDSHIP GENEROSITY

MOVEMENT 6
THE IMPACT OF YOUR LEGACY

- How did I build my legacy through my activities this week?

- Did I begin praying about who I want to bless after my time is over here on Earth?

- Have I started my estate plan? If not, what is the step I will take in the near future?

- How did I live this past week with the end in mind?

EPILOGUE

There are two life altering truths:

1. God is speaking.
2. You have one day fewer to listen than you had yesterday.

I rarely ever had those kinds of thoughts in my twenties and thirties, but now truths recur often. Have I listened to God? Have I really lived my life to the fullest? Have I heard God's voice?
The old adage is true: Our life is God's gift to us. What we do with it is our gift to God.

Jesus came to bring us rest if we will only stop long enough to listen and to let Him speak. This is the kind of life Jesus lived out in front of us. He connected with the Father intimately and dynamically. We, on the other hand, are often too busy doing things for God that we miss entirely the presence of God.

God really does have something to say to each one of us. I know it like the back of my Bible. I preach it, teach it, encourage others to listen, but if I'm not careful I'll get so focused my schedule that I don't slow down enough to hear the Whispers. When I shut down all the white noise and ambiance, God speaks. It's not always an audible voice, but a Voice just the same.

Every now and then I'll experience a feeling of being very small. You probably don't know what I'm talking about. All around me there are bigger ministries, larger budgets, more talented communicators, and more successful pastors. (I know you probably never feel that way, but may I confess that I do from time to time.) It's at that moment that I have to refocus on a simple four-word sentence, "Jesus is with me." I know. It's a Children's Sunday School sentence but it's still such a gigantic sentence. "Jesus is with me."

Jesus is with me, and He has something He wants to say *to* me —

not just *through* me. It's not enough for us to believe that He exists and has something to say to me personally. It would be a shame for us to finally arrive in Heaven and not recognize the voice of God. In order to hear Him, I must remember to adjust my spiritual sensors. It took me a while to grow out of the belief that He's not a manipulator of people and I don't have to be one either. We can't control our people. That's the way God made them: UNCONTROLABLE. Sometimes in the past I've wanted to, but I've gotten over it. These sheep can't be controlled, but they can be led. The basics of listening must overcome the relentless pressures that we as worship leaders and pastors face. Let me encourage you to try the following things that will lead to a heightened sensitivity to hear God's voice:

• *Today – I'll live a life of urgency and celebration. The brooding life is not holy. To many it might look holy, but a gravedigger and party pooper do not a Kingdom make!*

• *Today – I'll simplify to remove distractions. Our inability to hear God is directly linked to the static of modern life. It's perhaps the greatest plague of the church. We are uncomfortable with silence. The things we place before our eyes, the multitude of messages we receive on a daily basis, even the food that we eat potentially blocks our reception of God's voice. We often expel the voice of God through texts, emails, Facebook walls, radio, TV, and music.*

• *Today – I'll meditate on Holy Scripture. Don't just read it. Become preoccupied with it! Stuff yourself full of holy words and you'll see it bring a blessing of peace over your life because your eyes and ears are open to His Word.*

• *Today - I'll stop all self-promotion campaigns. We are all involved in a throne battle. Who will you place on the throne of your life? To which king will you bow down?*

- Today - I'll follow God's heart and not my own. Keep in mind what God thinks of your heart: It is deceitful. Songs, movies and pop culture have urged us to follow our heart. Please don't. It's a dead-end proposition. Discover the heart of God and follow His.

- Today - I'll clarify boundaries in my personal world. The ability to hear God is directly related to our ability to say no to lots of things in your life, even a few good things. We understand that we are not capable of doing everything for everybody. Your closest friends will not understand it. Some will be disappointed in you and others will think you are a prude, but celebrate your boundaries. If you understand the purpose you have been created to achieve, saying NO (sometimes in bold and all caps) is not just recommended, it is required.

- Today - I'll seek discernment regarding my day. Every morning, ask for wisdom and courage. You need them both in order to discern the voice of Holy God and to do whatever He tells you to do.

- Today - I won't tolerate negativity. If I find myself surrounded by negative, whiney, sarcastic people, I'll consider the floorplan of my life and think about doing a little renovation.

- Today - I'll have faith in the process. St. John of the Cross, an early church father, coined the term: the dark midnight of the soul. "The journey in Faith–the midnight of the soul when the light has all faded away and darkness has completely descended." He concludes that many Christ followers don't wish to endure the power of pain and tragedy that is necessary to pass through before the light shines again. I would argue that an overriding theme of the Bible is that suffering is not simply to be experienced but celebrated. It produces a deeper intimacy with God.

EPILOGUE

I hope that today is enough to lead you into a conversation with the Divine. He speaks softly and He speaks in present tense.

As we pursue to glorify God, we begin to understand the power of John the Baptist's vision statement. It's beautiful simplicity gives us a perfect understanding of what it means to give God glory. It's so straightforward and yet so beautifully challenging: *"He must increase, but I must decrease" (John 3:30)*. That's what it sounds like when we discover the glory of God.

It all comes down to this. There's going to be a celebration. One day every believer will be together. Paul, Moses, David, Barnabas, Noah, and Jesus and a billion or more of your closest friends. What we see now only in shadows, we will see face to face (1 Cor. 13:12). And at that moment when all the dreams come true, when our faith is realized, we will celebrate and review all God did in our lives and with the resources we give back to Him. Wouldn't it be a great idea to begin that celebration here on earth before we get to the ultimate celebration? Wouldn't it be great if, from the view of Heaven, we look back on our life on earth and realize that we gave our treasures away so we could have eternal treasures in Heaven? The truth is that often we're only thinking about the day in front of us. We may think it's all we have time to think about.

- Are we upside down on the truck?
- Do we have enough to go to Florida again this year?
- Will our team make it to the Super Bowl?

Think of Lordship as an investment in eternity. You are making investments as you follow Jesus by the influence you have on others, your generosity for the Kingdom, and how you live your life as an offering to God. Those deposits on a consistent basis are a statement of trust and faith in the Father.

At the grand award ceremony what words sound best?

Well done. You made it, even though you gave what you felt safe giving. You never stepped out of your comfort zone. You trusted in your ability to assure financial well-being. You had a really great time, and you saw some really great things.

Or

Well done. You radically followed Christ and it was reflected in every component of your life.

A radical pursuit of Lordship is arduous. This radical climb relentlessly challenges us to trust God in all areas of our lives, but the payoff far exceeds the pain. Paul reminds us, *"For I consider that the sufferings of this present time are not worth comparing with the glory that is going to be revealed to us"* (Rom. 8:18). In other words, there's no comparison. What we will experience through Lordship isn't even in the same area code as the life of a nominal believer. We get to revel in the glorious wonder of divine intimacy with Christ our King!

SPIRITUAL GIFTS INVENTORY

Here's a simple inventory which can help you consider the spiritual gifts you've been given.

Instructions: For each statement, rate yourself on a scale of 1 to 5:
1 = Strongly Disagree
2 = Disagree
3 = Neutral
4 = Agree
5 = Strongly Agree

Be honest with yourself and reflect on your natural inclinations, talents, and preferences.

Administration:
__ I enjoy organizing events and activities.
__ I am good at creating plans and schedules.
__ I find satisfaction in managing resources efficiently.
__ I am drawn to leadership roles.

Service:
__ I feel fulfilled when helping others practically.
__ I am sensitive to the needs of those around me.
__ I enjoy doing acts of kindness for people.
__ I am willing to give my time and energy to assist others.

Teaching:
__ I find joy in explaining concepts to others.
__ I am patient when helping others learn.
__ People often come to me for advice or guidance.
__ I am good at simplifying complex ideas.

Encouragement:
__ I naturally uplift and inspire those around me.

___ I am a good listener and empathetic towards others.
___ I enjoy giving words of affirmation.
___ I am skilled at cheering people up during difficult times.

Leadership:
___ I am comfortable leading in group settings.
___ Others often look to me for direction.
___ I am confident in making decisions.
___ I have a vision for how things could be improved.

Wisdom:
___ I tend to see situations from a broader perspective.
___ People often seek my counsel for important decisions.
___ I have a knack for offering practical solutions.
___ I am patient and thoughtful in my responses.

Hospitality:
___ I enjoy making people feel welcome and comfortable.
___ I am skilled at creating a warm and inviting atmosphere.
___ I like hosting events and gatherings at my home.
___ I am open to meeting new people and making connections.

Artistic Creativity:
___ I am drawn to artistic expression (music, painting, writing, etc.).
___ I find spiritual fulfillment through creative activities.
___ I am often inspired by beauty in the world around me.
___ I enjoy using my creativity to worship or praise.

Evangelism:
___ I am passionate about sharing my faith with others.
___ I am comfortable engaging in conversations about spirituality.
___ I find joy in helping others discover their faith.
___ I believe in the importance of spreading spiritual truth.

Prophecy:
___ I often have insights into spiritual truths.
___ I am unafraid to speak out about moral or ethical issues.
___ I feel a responsibility to challenge and inspire others.
___ I have a strong sense of discernment regarding right and wrong.

SPIRITUAL GIFTS INVENTORY

Faith:
_ I have a strong sense of trust in a God's guidance.
_ I am unshaken by difficult circumstances.
_ I often encourage others to trust in spiritual truths.
_ I find peace and comfort through my faith.

Giving:
_ I am generous with my resources, time, and talents.
_ I find joy in supporting charitable causes.
_ I am motivated to contribute to the well-being of others.
_ I see material possessions as a means to bless others.

Intercession:
_ I feel a strong urge to pray for others regularly.
_ I am sensitive to the spiritual needs of those around me.
_ I am moved to pray for situations beyond my personal concerns.
_ I believe in the power of prayer to bring about change.

LORDSHIP GENEROSITY

Results:

Add up your scores for each section to determine your potential spiritual gifts:

Administration: Total Score _____
Service: Total Score _____
Teaching: Total Score _____
Encouragement: Total Score _____
Leadership: Total Score _____
Wisdom: Total Score _____
Hospitality: Total Score _____
Artistic Creativity: Total Score _____
Evangelism: Total Score _____
Prophecy: Total Score _____
Faith: Total Score _____
Giving: Total Score _____
Intercession: Total Score _____

Keep in mind that this is just a simple example of a spiritual gifts inventory.

GROUP DISCUSSION GUIDE

The following discussion guide allows small groups to unpack the content of each movement. Feel free to pick just a few of the questions from each session. There's no need to answer them all. This allows you to customize the session to fit your group's life stages and personalities.

SESSION 1
THE BALANCE OF YOUR TIME

Our journey begins by looking at how we spend our time. We noted that the average American spends a significant amount of time watching television and staring at screens.

1. How do you manage your screen time, and do you think it reflects the lordship of Jesus?

2. How does the concept of time as a gift from God impact your perspective on how you use it?

3. How can we apply the principles of making the most of our time while maintaining a sense of purpose and serenity to our own lives?

4. In this chapter, Matt suggests using the "4W questions" (What, Where, Why, and Who) as a lens to examine how you spend your time. How might incorporating these questions into your daily routine help you establish your generosity of time and the lordship of Jesus?

5. The "P.E.O.P.L.E. plan" acronym is introduced for effective time management. Which aspect of this plan resonates most with you,

and how could you implement it in your daily life?

6. How can the principle of "Follow me" be applied to your approach to mentorship and investing in others?

7. Who in your life could benefit from your intentional discipleship, and how might you go about building that relationship?

8. How do you approach sharing your own experiences, including failures and adversities, to help others learn and grow?

9. Trusting the process of discipleship is highlighted as essential. How can you balance the patience required for long-term investment with the desire to see immediate results?

10. How do you identify and handle distractions or negative influences in your life, as illustrated by Nehemiah's response to opposition?

11. The chapter concludes with the story of Edward I. Try, highlighting the dangers of overcommitment and losing sight of one's true purpose. How do you find balance between serving and overwhelming yourself with responsibilities?

12. Reflect on the questions posed in the "Absolute Eternals" section. What actions are you taking in your life to foster generosity of time? How might you adjust your priorities to reflect the lordship of Jesus?

SESSION 2
THE EXPRESSION OF YOUR GIFTS

Before this session, complete the spiritual gifts assessment.

1. How does the analogy of the Body of Christ shape your understanding of the diversity and uniqueness of individual roles within the Church? How can this perspective impact how we view and interact with one another in your church?

2. This chapter emphasizes that each person is unique and has a specific purpose within the Body of Christ. How does the concept of being "destined to be where you are and when you are" affect your understanding of your own life circumstances and calling?

3. How have your past experiences shaped who you are today? How might they play a role in your future calling?

4. Dwight L. Moody's quote is highlighted: "The world has yet to see what God can do with someone who is fully consecrated to Him." What does it mean to be fully consecrated to God? How might this level of dedication impact the way we approach our calling and use our spiritual gifts?

5. Matt and G.B. point out that there are several ways to determine your spiritual gifts, including prayer, reflection on observations from others, and considering your Christ-like impulses during adversity. Which of these methods resonate with you the most, and why?

6. How can the gift of serving sometimes be underrated or undervalued? How can a person with the gift of serving contribute to the health and growth of a religious community?

GROUP DISCUSSION GUIDE

7. Reflecting on the scriptural references in this chapter, how does the concept of the diversity and distribution of spiritual gifts among believers contribute to the overall unity and strength of the Church?

8. In what ways can a person's spiritual gifts be aligned with their life's purpose and the mission of the Church? How can individuals and communities work together to ensure that everyone's unique gifts are utilized effectively for the common good?

9. Consider the concept of stewardship of spiritual gifts, as mentioned in 1 Peter 4:10-11. How does viewing your gifts as a form of stewardship influence your attitude and approach toward using them to serve others and to bring glory to God?

SESSION 3
THE STEWARDSHIP OF YOUR FINANCES

1. The passage from Mark 10:17-21 highlights Jesus challenging the rich man to give up his possessions and follow Him. How does this story illustrate the concept of Lordship? Why do you think Jesus often used money and possessions to test people's commitment?

2. Tithing is often seen as an expression of stewardship and obedience. How does the act of tithing reflect the understanding of God's ownership and authority over our lives and possessions?

3. How does tithing promote unity and shared purpose among church members? In what ways does tithing contribute to a thriving and vibrant church community?

4. Discuss the challenges and considerations associated with tithing. How can the principle of cheerful giving be emphasized in the context of tithing?

5. The reasons for giving a tithe outlined in the text include worship, promise, teaching, blessing, provision, investment, and more. Which of these reasons resonate most with you, and why? Are there any reasons you would add to the list based on your own beliefs and experiences?

6. The story of R.G. LeTourneau exemplifies extreme generosity and commitment to tithing. How can his story challenge our perspectives on giving and stewardship?

7. Tithing is described as a faith-building practice that strengthens one's trust in God. How does tithing challenge believers to step into a realm of faith and experience the supernatural? Have you

personally witnessed or experienced any instances of supernatural provision through tithing?

8. How does tithing affect one's attitude towards money and materialism? How can the act of tithing counteract the tendency to hold onto possessions tightly? In what ways does tithing cultivate a spirit of generosity and contentment?

9. Consider the statement that "tithing is a joy." How does giving with no regard for receiving contribute to a deeper sense of happiness and fulfillment? How can tithing transform our perspective on wealth accumulation and the true meaning of abundance?

10. Tithing is not only about financial giving but also about unity and shared commitment. How does tithing unify believers within a church community? How does it extend beyond individual actions to impact families and the broader body of believers?

11. Why do you think tithing can be contagious? How can the joy and transformation experienced through tithing inspire others to start giving? Can you share any personal stories of how your giving has inspired someone else?

12. Discuss the biblical foundations of tithing and the promises associated with it. How do passages such as Malachi 3:10 and 2 Corinthians 9:6-7 reinforce the idea of giving as a deeply rooted principle in Scripture? How does understanding the biblical basis of tithing influence your perspective on giving?

SESSION 4
THE CLEANING OF THE SLATE

True worship is more than just singing songs or attending church services; it's a reflection of our heart's posture toward God. Here are some discussion questions based on the content you provided for the chapter "The Cleaning of the Slate".

Initial Responses:
- Have you ever experienced a situation where a small issue escalated into a larger conflict? How did it affect relationships and the overall environment?
- How do you typically respond to insults or disagreements? Do you tend to hold onto resentment or seek resolution?

Resentments and Broken Fellowship:
- How does the analogy of a "root of bitterness" apply to unresolved resentment within a community or church?
- Can you think of any biblical examples where unresolved resentment or offense led to destructive consequences?

Rebellion and Like-Minded Rebels:
- Have you observed situations where people who feel offended or hurt gather like-minded individuals around them? What tends to be the outcome of such gatherings?
- How can this pattern of seeking out people who share similar resentments hinder the process of reconciliation?

Dealing with Resentment:
- Share examples of strategies or steps that can be taken to address resentment at an early stage before it escalates. How can these strategies be applied within a church or community context?
- What role does communication play in preventing resentment from growing into a larger conflict?

The Role of Rebels:
- Discuss the reasons why rebels may seek to draw others into their conflicts rather than addressing the issue directly with the person involved.

- How can church leaders or community members recognize when rebels are actively spreading dissent and divisiveness?

Intervention and Peacemaking:
- What qualities or characteristics make someone an effective peacemaker within a community or church setting?
- Share examples of situations where a private, closed-door intervention could potentially resolve conflicts more effectively than a public confrontation.

The Cost of Broken Fellowship:
- Reflect on the analogy of a broken bone that needs to be set in order to heal properly. How does this analogy apply to mending broken fellowship within a church or community?
- What challenges might leaders face when attempting to mend broken fellowships? How can these challenges be overcome?

Process of Personal Renewal: Mindfulness and Illumination:
- When was the last time you intentionally sought silence and stillness to listen to God's voice? How did that experience impact your perspective?
- How can the practice of mindfulness help individuals become more receptive to God's guidance and renewal?

Repentance and Forgiveness:
- Share your understanding of the difference between conviction and repentance. How does repentance involve both a change in understanding and a change in behavior?
- How can a call to repentance be seen as an invitation to life and restoration rather than as a condemnation?

Receiving and Offering Forgiveness:
- Have you ever struggled to accept forgiveness from God or from others even after repenting? How can a failure to receive forgiveness affect our spiritual well-being?
- Discuss the concept of forgiveness as a gift we give ourselves. How does forgiving someone free us from being anchored to the past?

- Extreme Forgiveness and Reflection of God's Character:

What impact does extreme forgiveness have on both the forgiver and the one forgiven? Share examples of situations where radical forgiveness transformed relationships.

- How does God's willingness to forgive us influence our willingness to forgive others, even in difficult circumstances?

Worship and Gratitude:

- How does releasing forgiveness create an atmosphere for genuine worship of God?
- Share personal experiences where practicing forgiveness led to a deeper sense of connection with God and a greater ability to worship Him.

These discussion questions aim to engage participants in thoughtful reflection and conversation about the chapter's themes of forgiveness, reconciliation, and personal renewal. Feel free to adapt and expand upon these questions based on the needs and dynamics of your discussion group.

SESSION 5
THE STORY OF YOUR LIFE

1. In the introduction, it's mentioned that each decision we make, every person we encounter, and every action we take contributes to the story of our lives. How does this concept resonate with you personally?

2. In this chapter, we read about the roles of different characters in stories, such as villains like Haman and guides like Mordecai. Can you identify characters from your own life who fit into these roles? How do they influence your personal narrative?

3. Mordecai plays a significant role as a guide to Esther, encouraging her to embrace her destiny and rise above her fears. Who are the Mordecai's in your life? How have they helped you navigate challenges or pursue opportunities?

4. Prayer is highlighted as a crucial aspect of the story, preceding action and inviting divine intervention. Do you have any experiences where prayer has played a significant role in shaping events or outcomes in your life?

5. The text discusses the concept of unexpected twists in stories, where circumstances suddenly change. Can you think of any unexpected twists or turning points in your own life story? How did you navigate them?

6. The characteristics of a glory giver are outlined towards the end of the chapter including:
surrender, passion for people, radical generosity, and extraordinary faith. How do these characteristics manifest in your life? Are there areas where you feel challenged to grow in these aspects?

7. We looked at the importance of giving glory to God rather than seeking glory for oneself. How do you interpret this distinction in your own life? How do you actively seek to glorify God in your actions and decisions?

8. Reflecting on the themes presented, what aspects of your own story do you feel inspired to change or enhance? How might you incorporate the lessons learned from characters like Esther, Mordecai, and the glory giver into your own narrative?

SESSION 6
THE IMPACT OF YOUR LEGACY

Farming and Estate Planning
- How does the chapter draw a parallel between farming and estate planning? What similarities do you see between these two processes?
- In the chapter, the author references 2 Corinthians 9:6-7, where the apostle Paul talks about sowing and reaping generously. How is this biblical principle related to estate planning and Lordship Generosity, and what implications does it have for your own financial planning?
- Tod highlights the importance of individual, heartfelt decisions in estate planning. Why is it emphasized that this is a personal choice rather than a decision made by a group or committee?

Who Needs an Estate Plan?
- What are some common misconceptions regarding estate planning?
- Have you held any of these misconceptions before?
- How can estate planning impact the well-being and future of your loved ones? Discuss the scenarios mentioned in the chapter and the potential consequences of not having an estate plan in place.

Section 3: What's in an Estate Plan?
Tod mentions the four essential documents in an estate plan: living will, medical power of attorney, financial power of attorney, and last will and testament.
- Do you have these documents in place or understand their importance in managing your affairs? Share your thoughts and experiences.

Benefits of an Estate Plan

Tod describes the benefits of estate planning, such as naming an executor, tax planning, and charitable giving. Which of these benefits resonate with you the most, and how might they influence your own estate planning decisions?

- In the chapter, the idea of tithing your estate to support Kingdom causes is discussed. How does this align with your personal values, and would you consider incorporating it into your estate plan?

Overcoming Fears

What are some of the fears or challenges people might face when it comes to estate planning? How can these be overcome, and what steps can individuals take to start their estate planning journey?

- In the Tod's conclusion, readers are encouraged to take steps toward building their estate plan. What are your next steps or action items, and who can you reach out to for guidance?

NOTES

1. Jerry Bridges, *The Gospel for Real Life : Turn to the Liberating Power of the Cross...Every Day* (Navpress Pub Group, 2002)

2. Peter Drucker, https://drucker.institute/thedx/youre-no-leader-at-least-not-without-practice/

LORDSHIP GENEROSITY

OUR TEAM

Matt Tullos served as primary writer for the contents of the book. He is Stewardship Specialist for the Tennessee Baptist Mission Board. In the past he has served on staff at LifeWay, Louisiana Baptists, and as Senior Pastor of Indian Lake Peninsula Church, in Hendersonville, TN. He has written 12 books including Aha Moments for Worship and Uh-Oh! Aha! and Glory Be! Matt has been married to Darlene Tullos since 1986. They are the parents of four sons: Isaac, Jacob, Nathan, and Caleb.

G.B. Howell helped shape the content, provided stories, original content, and ideas for Lordship Generosity. He was raised in South Georgia. He went to Carson-Newman College (now University) in Jefferson City, Tennessee, and majored in Religion. He attended Midwestern Baptist Theological Seminary in Kansas City, Missouri and received a Master of Divinity degree. He earned a Ph.D. in the Integration of Society and Religion from Oxford (now Omega) Graduate School in Dayton, Tennessee. He returned to Midwestern Seminary and received a Master of Arts in Biblical Archaeology. He went to LifeWay Christian Resources, where he was editor of Biblical Illustrator magazine, which explored Biblical archaeology, culture, history, geography, and Greek and Hebrew word studies. He also worked with the team that produced the CSB Holy Land Illustrated Bible.

Tod Tanner wrote the final chapter, "The Impact of Your Legacy." He has degrees from Texas A&M University, Southwestern Baptist Theological Seminary, and The Southern Baptist Theological Seminary. He has pastored churches in Texas and Tennessee. He and his family reside in Wartrace, TN and he is currently serving as the Executive Vice President of the Tennessee Baptist Foundation.

Tammy Harris served as editor for Lordship Generosity. Tammy was raised in Benton, Tennessee. She is an Administrative Assistant for the Tennessee Baptist Mission Board where she has served for 21+ years. She is a graduate of Cleveland State Community College and Middle Tennessee State University. Tammy has been a technical writer and has worked on a video crew for the Metro Nashville Network, previously the Government Access Channel. She also has a history in radio broadcasting. She and her husband, Kevin, live in Spring Hill, Tennessee.

Special thanks to **Dr. Randy C. Davis**, **Chris Turner**, **James Wilson**, **Trish Dubes** and **Tennessee Baptists**.

LORDSHIP GENEROSITY

Made in the USA
Columbia, SC
18 June 2025

59537589R00093